A LONGMAN
LATIN READER

CICERO AND SALLUST

On the Conspiracy of Catiline

Prepared by E. J. Barnes and John T. Ramsey

LONGMAN

Cicero and Sallust: On the Conspiracy of Catiline

Longman Inc., 95 Church Street, White Plains, N. Y. 10601

Associated companies:
Longman Group Ltd., London
Longman Cheshire Pty., Melbourne
Longman Paul Pty., Auckland
Copp Clark Pitman, Toronto
Pitman Publishing Inc., New York

Authors: **E. J. Barnes**, C. W. Jefferys Secondary School, North York, Ontario
John T. Ramsey, The University of Illinois at Chicago
Series Editor: **Professor Gilbert Lawall**, University of Massachusetts,
Amherst, Massachusetts
Consultants: **Jane Harriman Hall**, Mary Washington College,
Fredericksburg, Virginia
Richard A. LaFleur, University of Georgia,
Athens, Georgia
Robert E. Morse, Saint Andrew's School,
Boca Raton, Florida

Executive editor: Lyn McLean
Production editor: Elsa van Bergen
Text and cover designer: Gayle Jaeger
Production supervisor: Judith Stern

ISBN 0-582-36752-2

Compositor: r/tsi typographic company, inc.
Printer: R. R. Donnelley & Sons Company

88 89 90 91 92 9 8 7 6 5 4 3 2 1

CONTENTS

ACKNOWLEDGMENTS

We wish to express our thanks to the following persons: to the series editor, Professor Gilbert Lawall, for his tireless aid and guidance in pointing the way to a successful conclusion of our task; to Professor Michael Alexander of the University of Illinois at Chicago for advice on several historical matters and for technical assistance in connection with word processing; to Professor Elizabeth Gebhard and Professor Jack Davis, also of the University of Illinois, thanks to whose help it has been possible to include the sketch of the Roman Forum in Cicero's time drawn after the latest archaeological reports in Coarelli; and to Shirley Higginbotham and Cheryl Baunbach-Caplan, who typed the first draft of the introduction and the notes and text for lines 1–229. Finally, we thank our wives for the generous understanding with which they encouraged us in the preparation of this book.

E. J. Barnes
J. T. Ramsey

INTRODUCTION

For many centuries the story told here has been a constant favorite with students of Latin and those interested in Roman history. We have taken the unusual step, however, of telling the story by interweaving into a single fabric the accounts found in two of our chief ancient sources. The author of one of these sources, the consul Cicero, was himself a principal in the action; he is represented by excerpts from three powerful speeches he himself delivered during the course of the political struggle that is our theme. The other author, Sallust, was a historian who liked to see great events as reflections of the lives of the people who acted out these events. Together these two authors wrote enough material on the Catilinarian conspiracy to take up several books this size. Accordingly we have had to be selective. In making our selection, we have kept in mind above all that the modern student wants the story. "What happened next?" was our main concern, and it governed every choice of text and of pictorial materials. The Latin text comprising each selection is unaltered and unabridged. The boldfaced Arabic numbers affixed to the text signify the source within each work as a whole by chapter number for Sallust and section number for the speeches of Cicero.

CONCERNING THE CATILINARIAN CONSPIRACY

The main events covered in this volume took place in 63 B.C., the year in which the distinguished Roman orator Cicero was consul. The historian Sallust, born in 86 B.C., was twenty-three years old at the time. Sallust was, therefore, conceivably a firsthand observer of many of the events that took place, although he gives no indication in his account of the conspiracy that he actually was, and we have no concrete evidence for assuming that he was present in Rome or even in Italy during this year. Certainly, however, Sallust was acquainted with many of the figures involved in these momentous events. When he came to write his account of the conspiracy some twenty years after it had occurred (perhaps publishing his monograph in 44 or 43 B.C.), he could draw upon an abundance of both written and oral sources.

The ringleader of the plot formed against the Roman government in 63 B.C. was the nobleman Lucius Sergius Catilina, commonly known now as Catiline. Catiline was born into an old patrician family that had produced consuls and had been prominent in the fifth and fourth centuries B.C. but had not played an active role in Roman politics for many generations. Since we know that Catiline was praetor in 68 B.C., for which a candidate had to be at least thirty-nine years of age, we can place his date of birth no later than 108 B.C. Catiline was, therefore, at least two years older than Cicero, who was born in 106. If he had succeeded in reaching the consulship immediately after the two-year interval that had to elapse between the praetorship and consulship, he would have been consul in 65. We know, in fact, that Catiline

1

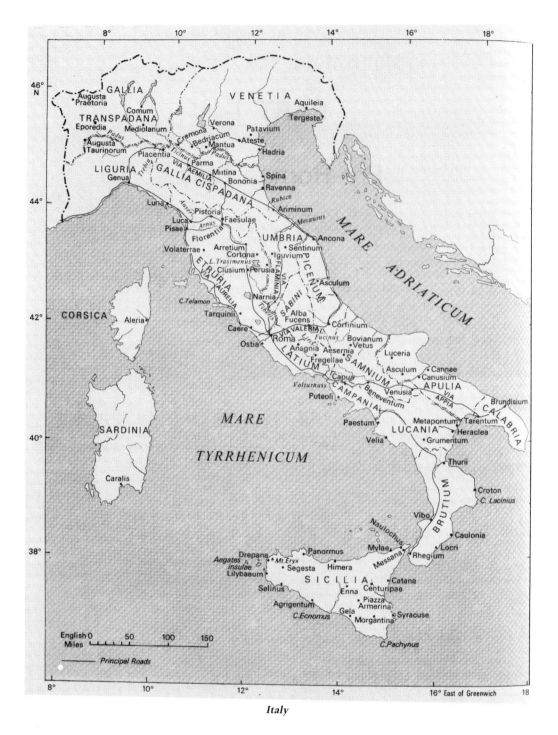

Italy

attempted to stand for election in 66, but his candidacy was disallowed by the magistrate who presided over the elections, apparently on the ground that Catiline was soon to face criminal charges arising out of his administration of the province of Africa in 67 where he had been governor. This trial for extortion took place in 65 and resulted in an acquittal, not without the claim that the verdict had been rigged, but it served to delay Catiline's candidacy for one more year.

Sallust takes Catiline's candidacy for the consulship in 64 as the starting point for his narrative of the conspiracy proper. He presents Catiline as

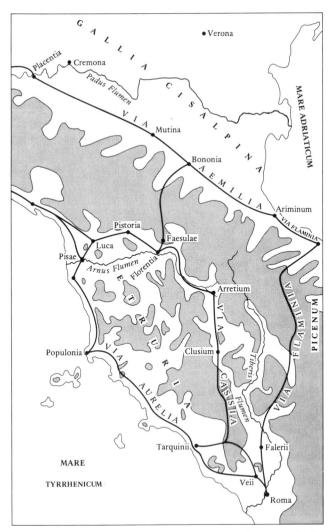

Northern Italy (shaded areas show elevations above 600 feet)

outlining to his supporters in a speech before the elections a plot to massacre their political enemies, to seize choice offices and appointments for themselves in a bloody uprising, and to remedy their financial difficulties by cancelling all outstanding personal debts. However, contrary to the impression given by Sallust, Catiline is unlikely to have advocated such radical measures in 64. We know from other sources that Catiline enjoyed the backing of several wealthy and powerful politicians in this campaign. We also know that at his trial in 65, many reputable ex-consuls had testified for him and worked for his acquittal. Since he enjoyed the support of so many respectable political leaders in this period, he cannot have been viewed as a revolutionary troublemaker by the establishment.

The hope of Catiline's backers in 64 seems to have been to secure his election along with Gaius Antonius. Catiline and Antonius would then work as consuls in 63 for the passage of several radical legislative proposals, including a bill to relieve a debt crisis and a bill to settle the urban poor on parcels of public land. As proconsuls in 62, Catiline and Antonius would then proceed to govern the provinces of Cisalpine Gaul in northern Italy and

Macedonia. Both provinces contained Roman armies, and as the commanders of these military forces Catiline and Antonius would provide a useful counterbalance to the Roman general Gnaeus Pompey, who was expected to return to Italy from Asia with his army within the next year or two. Those politicians who feared or resented the influence of Pompey may have looked to Catiline and Antonius as useful allies in the future if political rivalries led to armed confrontation. People living in Rome could vividly recall how twenty years earlier the general Lucius Cornelius Sulla had returned with his army from Asia and seized control of the Roman government in a civil war.

Events, however, took a different course. Cicero, despite the disadvantage of being the first in his family to hold political office, managed to alarm the voters against his two chief rivals, Catiline and Antonius, with the result that Cicero and Antonius were elected consuls for 63. Cicero effectively used his oratorical skills in the first half of 63 to defeat the radical legislative proposals that were brought before the assembly. By agreeing to exchange the provinces that had been assigned to them by lot for the following year, Cicero managed to detach his colleague Antonius from Catiline and so neutralize the threat posed by having a potential supporter of Catiline at the head of the government. Catiline revived his candidacy in 63 for 62, but in this year there is no evidence that he enjoyed the backing of influential supporters. To compensate for the loss of support in higher places, Catiline appears to have directed his appeal more and more to the down and out, those who had burdened themselves with debt and those who had suffered from the upheavals caused by the civil war with Sulla twenty years before. Cicero, meanwhile, recruited spies among Catiline's followers, as Sallust reports, to keep abreast of Catiline's schemes, and he actively worked for Catiline's defeat in the consular elections. In the end, the two candidates elected for 62 were L. Licinius Murena and D. Iunius Silanus.

Catiline's defeat for the consulship in 63 virtually exhausted all hope he might have had of achieving power by legitimate means. During the latter half of 63, therefore, Catiline began to organize his supporters in Rome and Italy with a view to bringing about a violent overthrow of the government. An ex-officer in Sulla's army, Gaius Manlius, was sent to the town of Faesulae, north of Rome in Etruria near modern Florence, to recruit an army. In Rome Catiline laid plans to bring about the assassination of Cicero and other political opponents. Among his chief lieutenants were the patricians Gaius Cornelius Cethegus, a young hotheaded senator, and Publius Cornelius Lentulus, who as one of the eight praetors was a high elected official of the government in 63.

Although rumors of the activities of Manlius in Etruria caused some alarm in the capital (in late October watches were posted in the city and the Senate granted extraordinary powers to Cicero and his colleague to protect the state), it was difficult for Cicero to proceed against Catiline and his associates for lack of concrete evidence. Finally on the night of 8–9 November, after the adjournment of a stormy meeting of the Senate and a failed attempt to assassinate Cicero on the morning of the seventh, Catiline departed from Rome to join his army at Faesulae. According to our sources, his departure was hastened by frustration at his lack of success in bringing about the removal of Cicero, and he wanted to strengthen his army and march against the city of Rome before the government gained time to recruit troops to put down the planned rebellion. Once Catiline had openly revealed his intention to wage war against his country by joining the forces at Faesulae,

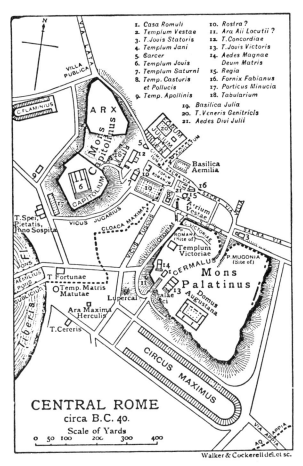

CENTRAL ROME

circa B.C. 40.

Scale of Yards

0   50   100   200   300   400

Walker & Cockerell del. et sc.

the Senate declared Catiline and Manlius outlaws and instructed the consuls to levy an army and take the field. This action was taken about mid-November. Meanwhile, after Catiline's departure from Rome, his associate, the praetor Lentulus, directed the activities of the conspirators who had remained behind. Upon a prearranged signal, after Catiline had brought his army south from Faesulae to the vicinity of Rome, they were to set fires at designated places in the city, and under the confusion caused by the fires and the darkness of night they were to begin the massacre of their political opponents. Catiline's army would then march into the city and complete the revolution.

As it turned out, the state was spared this upheaval by the vigilance of Cicero and the fortuitous seizure of some incriminating documents in December. These documents fell into the hands of the government when Cicero arranged for certain foreign ambassadors who had had dealings with the conspirators to be arrested. Lentulus, Cethegus, and some of the other chief figures of the conspiracy had attempted to recruit support for their cause from a Gallic nation, the Allobroges. The Allobroges, however, betrayed the plans of the conspirators to Cicero, and with their help Cicero managed to secure written evidence of the involvement of Lentulus, Cethegus, and some others in a plot to overthrow the government. On the strength of this evidence, five of the leading conspirators still in Rome were sentenced to death by the Senate and executed on 5 December.

When news of these executions reached Catiline's camp, his army began to melt away, since it appeared that he could no longer count upon an

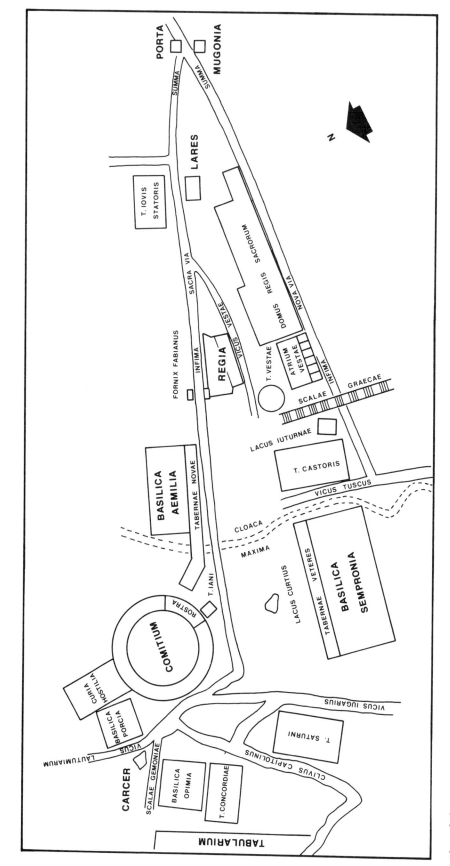

Plan of the Roman Forum in Cicero's time

6

uprising in the city to aid the assault by his army. Furthermore, by mid-December, armies under the command of the consul Antonius and praetor Metellus Celer were beginning to hem in Catiline and his rebel forces in the north of Italy. After a desperate attempt to elude the government armies and march northward out of Italy into Gaul, Catiline drew up his army in early January of 62 near Pistoria in Etruria to face the legions of his former ally Antonius. The consul turned over the command of his troops to his second-in-command on the day of the battle rather than come face-to-face with his old comrade. Catiline's forces were outnumbered by perhaps more than five to one, but according to all accounts, they fought bravely and died almost to a man. The dead body of Catiline was found where the fighting had been most intense, and his head was cut off and sent to Rome as proof of his destruction.

So ended a remarkable chapter in Roman history. With some justification Cicero boasted at the time and later that he had saved the Roman state from destruction with a minimum of upheaval. What might have turned into a bloody civil war ended in such a fashion that Cicero could style it a "civil plot" (**cīvīlis coniūrātiō**) rather than a full-scale war.

ABOUT THE AUTHORS

Cicero

Marcus Tullius Cicero, a native of the Italian town of Arpinum, was born in 106 B.C. Although he was the first in his family to hold political office at Rome and therefore labored under the disadvantage of being a "new man" (**novus homō**), he rose steadily up the ladder of political offices (**cursus honōrum**). Beginning with the quaestorship in 75 B.C., which entitled him to a permanent seat in the Senate, he held each higher office in the first year he was eligible to do so according to the minimum-age requirement. His accomplishment of being elected consul for 63 is all the more remarkable when it is noted that Cicero is the only **novus homō** known to have reached this office, despite having no senatorial ancestors, during the period 93 to 48 B.C.

Clearly, it was Cicero's skill as a public speaker that enabled him to overcome the disadvantage of his birth into a nonsenatorial family. Cicero was recognized in his lifetime as Rome's foremost orator, and no other figure before or after him comes close to challenging his preeminence. We have preserved for us more speeches by Cicero than by any other classical Latin writer. Four of these speeches, the so-called *Catilinarians*, were composed at the time of the crisis caused by Catiline's conspiracy and published a few years after the event. These four speeches and several others, most notably the *Pro Murena* also of 63 and the *Pro Sulla* of 62, shed valuable light on the events and personalities connected with the conspiracy.

In later years, Cicero took what some have regarded as excessive pride in his accomplishment of saving the state from Catiline's plot. Cicero paid a price for his stern measures against the conspirators, when in 58 B.C. his political enemy Publius Clodius caused him to be sent into exile from Italy for more than a year on the grounds that he had illegally executed Lentulus, Cethegus, and the three other conspirators who were put to death without a trial. Although Cicero was recalled from exile in 57, he was not able at that time to play the leading role in politics that he craved. As a **novus homō**, he remained an object of jealousy to the old, established families, and he lacked the network of political connections and allies to influence the course of events as he would have liked.

When the civil war between Caesar and Pompey broke out in 49, Cicero joined Pompey but put no great trust in either side to use victory wisely. After the triumph of Caesar, Cicero's life was spared, but he was inevitably forced into virtual retirement from political life. Ironically, it was twenty years after his consulship that Cicero once again briefly assumed the direction of the Roman government. In the turmoil that followed the assassination of Julius Caesar in March of 44 B.C., Cicero was increasingly drawn back into an active role in politics. During 43, as a senior ex-consul, he became the spokesman and leader of the group that tried but failed to restore the Republic. He fell as one of the first victims in December 43 B.C. in the purge carried out by Mark Antony and Caesar's young grandnephew Octavian, who was later (in 27 B.C.) to assume the title Augustus and rule as the first Roman emperor.

Sallust

Gaius Sallustius Crispus, commonly known as Sallust, was born, as nearly as we can tell, in 86 B.C. and came from the Sabine town of Amiternum. He was, therefore, some twenty years younger than Cicero, and, like Cicero, he belonged to that class of **novī hominēs** whose ambition led them to a career in Roman politics. Sallust first comes to our notice in 52 B.C., when as one of the ten tribunes of the people he was a leader in the faction that pressed for the condemnation of Cicero's client Titus Annius Milo for the murder of Cicero's old political adversary Publius Clodius. Although Cicero and Sallust found themselves on opposite sides in this bitterly contested case, there is a tradition that the two men afterwards reconciled their differences.

Sallust's career, however, did not prosper. Removed from the Senate by the censors in 50 B.C., Sallust sought refuge in the camp of Julius Caesar, who was nearing the end of his term as governor of the two Gauls. When civil war broke out in the following year, Sallust operated for a time at the head of one of Caesar's legions but was outmaneuvered by Pompey's generals. Three years later, however, in 46 B.C., Sallust held the praetorship and served with distinction in Caesar's African campaign against the remaining Republican forces under Cato. Following Caesar's victory in this war, Sallust was made the governor of a new province in Africa that Caesar created after the conquest of what had formerly been the Kingdom of Numidia. Our sources tell us that Sallust took advantage of this appointment to line his pockets, and although he was saved from prosecution upon his return to Rome in late 45 B.C. or early 44—perhaps thanks to the influence of Caesar—he was compelled to enjoy his ill-gotten gains in enforced retirement from politics.

During the next decade, from approximately 44 B.C. to his death in about 35, Sallust devoted himself to the writing of history. His first essay was the monograph on Catiline's conspiracy; this was followed a year or two later by a monograph on Rome's war in Africa with the Numidian prince Jugurtha (112–105 B.C.), and then Sallust turned to the more ambitious project of composing a history of the times following the dictatorship of Sulla. This latter work, known as the *Historiae*, was issued in five books and survives only in fragments. It covered the years 78 B.C. to approximately 67, and it is generally agreed that the composition of this work was broken off by the death of the author before he had reached his intended point of completion.

None of the Latin authors who composed histories before Sallust earned lasting recognition. Cicero dismisses this group as mere "chroniclers of events" (**nārrātōrēs rērum**) rather than true historians in a class with the

8

Greek writers Herodotus and Thucydides. Sallust was the first Latin writer to achieve fame as both a historian and a major prose stylist. In developing his distinctive style, Sallust aimed for a flavor reminiscent of the fifth-century Athenian historian Thucydides (ca. 460/55–400 B.C.). To capture in Latin some of the qualities for which the style of Thucydides was noted, such as rapidity, abruptness, and a fondness for poetical words and unusual grammatical constructions, Sallust consciously rejected the polished periodic Latin of Cicero and sought inspiration instead from the archaic prose of Rome's early annalists. One of these writers, Cato the Elder (234–149 B.C.), who in the second century B.C. was the first author to compose a history of Rome in Latin, proved an ideal model. The archaic and poetical flavor that Sallust achieved by drawing upon this source enabled him to fashion a new and distinctive prose that seemed ideally suited to the writing of history. The recognition that Sallust achieved as both a prose stylist and as historian may be judged by the fact that soon after his death he, like Cicero and later the poets Vergil and Horace, came to be considered a standard author in the school curriculum.

STYLISTIC TERMS

Style is the term used to identify the manner in which an author writes a work. The elements that make up an author's style are numerous, and different authors combine these elements in different ways and different proportions. The following list presents most of the stylistic features used by the two authors represented in this book and commented upon in the notes, where the terms are italicized at their first occurrence. (Numbers refer to lines of text and the related note.)

Alliteration is the effect created when two or more words in succession (or at short intervals) begin with the same letter or sound (34).

Allusion is a reference to some factor outside the actual piece of writing; allusions create associations for the reader that deepen the reader's appreciation of the work. So lines 121–122: **P. Scīpiō, pontifex . . ., Gracchum . . . prīvātus interfēcit.**

Anaphora is the repetition of a key word or phrase (108–110).

Antithesis brings words or ideas into contrast by balancing them against each other (292).

Archaism is the use of old-fashioned or obsolete language to lend a flavor of "old times" to a writer's style (1).

Assonance is a similarity of vowel sounds in adjacent words in which the consonants may differ. So line 37: **stīpendia pendere.**

Asyndeton (Greek, "unconnected") is a figure in which coordinated elements lack a connective, as in "I came, I saw, I conquered." See 91–94.

Chiasmus is the interlocking of pairs of words by arranging the second pair in reverse order: **a b b a**, as in "I cannot dig, to beg I am ashamed." See 10–11.

Climax (also called *crescendo*) occurs when words, phrases, or clauses in a series are arranged in ascending order of emphasis or expressiveness (424).

Convention is a device, technique, or practice that the writer selects from accepted precedents or tradition.

Epigram is a terse, pointed statement that says much in few words. So line 32: **nam idem velle atque idem nōlle, ea dēmum firma amīcitia est.**

Epithet is a modifier that expresses a quality or attribute that carries special significance (360).

Figurative language is the fanciful use of words so as to imply more than the literal meaning. Figures of speech add clarity, interest, and meaning. Some figures of speech are *pun, metaphor, simile,* and *hyperbole.*

Hendiadys is the expression of a more complex idea by the use of two words connected by "and," as in "gold and trinkets." See 345.

Hyperbole is the Greek word for overstatement or exaggeration (61).

Inversion is the deliberate changing of the natural order of words in a sentence. So line 15: **Agitābātur magis magisque in diēs animus ferōx**.

Irony is a use of words that suggest (sometimes in a humorous or mocking way) a meaning that is opposite to the meaning the words carry literally (118).

Juxtaposition is the placing side-by-side of two terms to create an association in the reader's mind. So lines 28–29: **neque ego . . . aut vāna ingenia incerta prō certīs captārem**.

Litotes is a form of understatement in which a sense is conveyed by the negative of its opposite, as in "not unwilling." So line 55: **nātus haud obscūrō locō**.

Metaphor is a type of comparison in which one idea is conveyed through another; in metaphor only half the comparison is made, and the rest is left to the imagination (174).

Metonymy (Greek, "change of name") is the substitution of the name of one object for that of a related object, as in "the American Eagle" instead of "the United States." See 352.

Pathos is that quality in a work that arouses feelings of pity or sadness in the reader (381–382).

Personification occurs when an abstract concept or inanimate object is given the attributes of persons (448; see also lines 50–51).

Realism is the depiction in writing of anything as it is in actuality (375–378).

Rhetorical is a term applied to a form of speech that in any way moves outside the limits of the plain and unadorned.

Rhetorical question is a question asked not for information but to create an effect (286).

Structure is the layout, architecture, or overall design given to a work.

Style is the manner of writing used by a writer. Style is individual to an author and is the sum of such features as choice of words, rhythms, mood, structure, figures, and other effects peculiar to the writer's work.

Symmetry is the careful balancing of elements of expression, like the sides of an equation. So lines 106–108: **Quō ūsque tandem abūtēre . . . ? Quam diū . . . ēlūdet? Quem ad fīnem . . . iactābit audācia?**

Synecdoche is the stating of part to represent the whole, as "fifty sail" to mean "fifty ships." See 160.

Theme is the central or overall idea of a work.

Tmesis is the division of a compound word into its separate parts by an intervening word or words. So **priusquam** in line 3: **prius explānanda sunt quam**.

Tone is the collective sense we have of a writer's attitude to the work, to its theme, or even to the reader.

Understatement is a form of assertion that states less than it suggests; understatement is the opposite of exaggeration (*hyperbole*). So lines 52–53: **Haec ipsa, ut spērō, vōbīscum ūnā cōnsul agam.**

Zeugma is a figure of speech in which a verb or adjective is set in relation to two nouns at once; it applies strictly to the one noun, but merely suggests the word that properly applies to the other. So we might say, "with weeping eyes and hearts" (where "grieving hearts" might be more appropriate). See line 52: **neque animus neque corpus ā vōbīs aberit** (here **corpus aberit** is realistic, but **animus aberit** is figurative).

THE STRUCTURE OF ROMAN SPEECHES

The structure and style of forensic speeches had been worked out in careful detail by Greek and Roman orators. Several ancient textbooks on speech making have survived.

Each section of a speech had its own particular function and character, and each was given a technical name. The names are all Latin terms. This shows that the study of oratory (which the Greeks called rhetoric) had become a Roman interest. It was, in fact, the basis in the Roman world of what we would call higher education. Cicero was considered by most Romans to be the foremost public speaker of his day.

A standard pattern for the structure of a speech was followed by all forensic speakers, and it may be outlined as follows:

1. **exōrdium** ("beginning"): the introduction
2. **nārrātiō** ("relating"): the outline of the facts of the case
3. **prōpositiō** ("setting forth"): the speaker's statement of what he intends to argue (later the word **prōpositiō** also came to mean the statement of a question of law or a case submitted for legal opinion)
4. **argūmentātiō** ("presentation of proofs"), consisting of two subsections:
   a. **cōnfirmātiō** ("making firm"): the arguments and facts for the speaker's case
   b. **refūtātiō** ("driving back"): the arguments and evidence against the opponent's case
5. **perōrātiō** ("speaking through to the end"): the recapitulation and closing of the speech

In the excerpts of speeches contained in this book, not all the above sections of any one speech are represented. Some speeches, in fact, did not contain all these sections; a **contiō** before the assembled populace would be of this shorter type. The selections presented in this book from the various speeches do, however, conform to the standard pattern as follows:

1. Speech of Catiline to his conspirators (early June, 64 B.C.): **exōrdium**, lines 26–32; **prōpositiō**, lines 33–47; **perōrātiō**, lines 48–54
2. Cicero, *First Speech Against Catiline*, to the Senate (8 November 63 B.C.): **exōrdium**, lines 106–130; **nārrātiō**, lines 131–156; **perōrātiō**, lines 157–164
3. Cicero, *Third Speech Against Catiline*, to the people (3 December 63 B.C.): **nārrātiō**, lines 192–215
4. Speech of Caesar to the Senate (5 December 63 B.C.): **exōrdium**, lines 263–267; **refūtātiō**, lines 268–291; **perōrātiō**, lines 292–296
5. Cicero, *Fourth Speech Against Catiline*, to the Senate (5 December 63 B.C.): **nārrātiō**, lines 297–316; **cōnfirmātiō**, lines 317–325; **perōrātiō**, lines 326–344
6. Speech of Cato to the Senate (5 December 63 B.C.): **prōpositiō**, lines 345–351; **refūtātiō**, lines 352–365; **perōrātiō**, lines 366–370

1 ***coniūrātiō, coniūrātiōnis** (f), conspiracy, plot. ***quam** (adv.), as . . . as possible (modifying **vērissumē**). **vērissumē**: this *archaic* spelling of the superlative is the one preferred by Sallust. Not only will *u* be found consistently for *i* in the suffix **-issumus**, but it appears as well in irregular superlatives, e.g., **maxuma** (12), and in such forms as **pulcherrumum** (30). **paucīs**: supply **verbīs** (ablative of means), "succinctly." **absolvō, absolvere** (3), **absolvī, absolūtum** (+ **dē** + abl.), to give an account (of).

2 ***facinus, facinoris** (n), deed, enterprise, (more commonly with a negative connotation) crime. ***in prīmīs**: = **imprīmīs** (adv.), especially, above all. **memorābilis, -is, -e**, memorable, remarkable. **memorābile**: predicate adjective modifying the object of **exīstumō**. **exīstumō**: = **exīstimō**; to lend an archaic flavor to his prose, Sallust consciously revived the older spelling using *u* in certain words that by his day were regularly spelled with an *i*. Other examples are furnished by **lubet** (9) for **libet** and **lubīdō** (12) for **libīdō**. ***scelus, sceleris** (n), crime, villainy, wickedness.

3 **novitās, novitātis** (f), novelty, unheard of nature. **novitāte**: causal ablative. **Dē cuius hominis**: the relative pronoun is here coordinating (= **Et dē eius**); the noun **hominis** is expressed to make it clear that **cuius** refers to **Catilīnae** at the head of the previous sentence. **explānō** (1), to make clear.

4 ***nārrō** (1), to relate. **faciam**: the subjunctive after **prius . . . quam** (split by *tmesis*) is related to the subjunctive of purpose and may be viewed as anticipatory; i.e., here the ideas of "before I embark upon" and "so that I may embark upon" are virtually one and the same.

5 **nōbilī genere**: ablative of source with **nātus**. Catiline belonged to an old patrician family that had produced consuls but not for over 300 years. These consular ancestors made Catiline **nōbilis** by birth. **vī . . . ingeniō** (6): supply **vir** with these ablatives of description.

6 ***ingenium, -ī** (n), inborn nature, character, talent. **prāvus, -a, -um**, vicious, depraved. **ab adulēscentiā**: born no later than 108 B.C., Catiline saw service in Rome's war to crush the revolt of her Italian allies (91—89 B.C.). He is also credited with playing an active role in the atrocities and purges that followed Lucius Cornelius Sulla's victory in a civil war later in the decade, when Sulla made himself dictator (82—79 B.C.). **intestīnus, -a, -um**, domestic (in contrast with foreign wars).

7 ***rapīna, -ae** (f), plundering. **discordia, -ae** (f), dissension. ***cīvīlis, -is, -e**, of a citizen (citizens), civil. **fuēre**: = **fuērunt**. Sallust nearly always wrote the archaic and poetical **-ēre** for the 3rd person plural of the perfect active indicative in preference to the standard prose form in **-ērunt**. **ibi**: = **in eīs**, i.e., the activities just enumerated. **iuventūs, iuventūtis** (f), youth, early manhood.

8 **patiēns**: supply the verb **erat** here and below after **animus** (9) and **ārdēns** (10). How would the meaning of **patiēns** be altered if its objects were in the accusative rather than the genitive? **inedia, -ae** (f), lack of food, fasting. **algor, algōris** (m), cold. ***vigilia, -ae** (f), lack of sleep, wakefulness. **crēdibilis, -is, -e**, capable of being believed, credible. **crēdibile**: with **cuiquam** (dative).

9 **subdolus, -a, -um**, crafty, deceitful. ***varius, -a, -um**, diverse, varied, versatile. **quīlibet, quaelibet, quodlibet**, whatever you please, any. **cuius . . . lubet**: here the compound word is split into two parts (tmesis), and the older spelling in **-lubet** is adopted. Construe with **reī**, an objective genitive governed by **simulātor** and **dissimulātor**. **simulātor, simulātōris** (m), one who puts on a pretense. This and the following noun, **dissimulātor, dissimulātōris** (m), "one who practices concealment," stand in apposition to **animus** and are equivalent to adjectives here: "capable of any pretense or concealment."

10 ***adpetēns, adpetentis** (+ gen.), covetous (of), greedy (for). **profūsus, -a, -um** (+ gen.) **suī**, "his own property"), lavish, prodigal with. **ārdēns, ārdentis**, fiery, ardent, eager. **cupiditās, cupiditātis** (f), desire, lust, craving. **satis . . . parum** (11): when an author wants to contrast two pairs of words, frequently he presents the words in each pair in reverse order (here, nominative genitive, answered by genitive nominative). This figure is known as *chiasmus*, and the word order alone makes the contrast sufficiently clear so that an adversative conjunction such as **sed** need not be expressed in Latin but is to be supplied in translation.

11 **sapientia, -ae** (f), wisdom, soundness of judgment. What use of the genitive with **parum**? **parum** (n indeclinable), an insufficient amount, too little. As the predicate supply **eī erat**. **vāstus, -a, -um**, desolate, immense, insatiable. **inmoderātus, -a, -um**, extravagant. ***nimis** (adv.), too, too much.

12

THE ACCOUNTS

SALLUST'S *BELLUM CATILINAE*

Sallust announces his intention to relate the conspiracy formed by the nobleman Catiline to overthrow the government of Rome.

[4.] Dē Catilīnae coniūrātiōne quam vērissumē poterō paucīs absolvam; nam id facinus in prīmīs ego memorābile exīstumō sceleris atque perīculī novitāte. Dē cuius hominis mōribus pauca prius explānanda sunt quam initium nārrandī faciam.

Endowed with great powers of physical endurance and a fondness for turmoil and bloodshed, Catiline was careless of how he managed his personal finances and set his sights on becoming master of Rome.

5　[5.] L. Catilīna, nōbilī genere nātus, fuit magnā vī et animī et corporis, sed ingeniō malō prāvōque. Huic ab adulēscentiā bella intestīna, caedēs, rapīnae, discordia cīvīlis grāta fuēre, ibique iuventūtem suam exercuit. Corpus patiēns inediae, algōris, vigiliae, suprā quam cuiquam crēdibile est. Animus audāx, subdolus, varius, cuius reī lubet simulātor ac dissimulātor,
10　aliēnī adpetēns, suī profūsus; ārdēns in cupiditātibus; satis ēloquentiae, sapientiae parum. Vāstus animus inmoderāta, incrēdibilia, nimis alta semper cupiēbat. Hunc post dominātiōnem L. Sullae lubīdō maxuma invāserat reī pūblicae capiundae, neque id quibus modīs adsequerētur, dum sibi rēgnum parāret, quicquam pēnsī habēbat.

1. What two qualities did Sallust aim for in his account of the conspiracy? (1)
2. Why did Sallust consider the conspiracy a suitable subject for his history? (2–3)
3. In what activities did Catiline spend his youth? (6–7)
4. What powers of physical endurance did Catiline possess? (8)
5. What kind of mind did Catiline possess? (9–10)
6. What event in Roman history inspired Catiline to aim for absolute power? (12–13)

---

12 *dominātiō, dominātiōnis (f), tyranny, despotism. *lubīdō, lubīdinis (f), desire, lust, passion.
13 *invādō, invādere (3), invāsī, invāsum, to enter, assail, come over. reī pūblicae capiundae: an objective genitive to be construed with lubīdō (12). Capiundae is an older spelling of the gerundive; -und-, in place of -end-, is the spelling Sallust adopted for the gerund and gerundive of 3rd conjugation verbs. adsequor, adsequī (3), adsecūtus sum, to attain, achieve. The object of this verb is id. dum = *dum modo, "provided that," "if only," introducing a clause of proviso, hence the subjunctive parāret (14).
14 *pēnsum, -ī (n) (*from the perfect passive participle of the verb* pendō), a thing weighed. quicquam pēnsī: partitive genitive; this is the predicate accusative of the verb habēbat, whose object is the indirect question id . . . adsequerētur (13). Translate, "a matter of importance."

15 *agitō (1) (*frequentative of* agō), to rouse, excite. *in diēs: this expression and cōtīdiē both mean "daily," but in diēs is employed with comparatives and expressions denoting increase or the opposite. *ferōx, ferōcis, fierce, savage.

16 cōnscientia, -ae (f), consciousness, conscience. quae utraque: = quārum utramque. The antecedents of the relative pronoun are inopiā (15) and cōnscientiā (16). ars, artis (f), skill, art, practice.

17 *memorō (1), to mention, relate. Incitābant: supply animum ferōcem or Catilīnam as the object of this verb. corruptus, -a, -um, decayed, decadent, depraved. quōs: the antecedent is the word mōrēs alone without its modifier. Translate "the decadent condition of the state's morality."

18 dīvorsa inter sē: in what sense can lūxuria and avāritia be viewed as "mutually opposed"? The spelling dīvorsa for dīversa is a conscious archaism. In the same manner Sallust writes, e.g., vostra (26) for vestra. lūxuria, -ae (f), extravagance, luxury. avāritia, -ae (f), covetousness, greed, avarice. *vexō (1), to harass, trouble, disturb.

19 simul . . . et: "both . . . and," joining the two quod clauses. *aes aliēnum, aeris aliēnī (n), debt, indebtedness (lit., copper—hence money—not one's own). omnīs: accusative plural; in both Sallust and Cicero, -īs, rather than -ēs, is the regular spelling in the masculine and feminine accusative plural of 3rd declension adjectives that have -ium in the genitive plural, and of i-stem nouns, e.g., montīs (61) and noctīs (94). ingēns, ingentis, huge, enormous.

20 plērīque: "many," "great numbers of," rather than "most." Sullānus, -a, -um, of Sulla, the Roman general and dictator (82–79 B.C.). largius, too lavishly, too freely. This adverb is to be taken closely with ūsī (+ ablative suō).

21 veteris: i.e., now nearly twenty years in the past, reckoning from 82 B.C. *memor, memoris, remembering, mindful.

22 nūllus exercitus: normally in peacetime no army was stationed permanently in Italy south of the province of Cisalpine Gaul, which embraced the northern region between the Apennines and the Alps (see map, p. 3). Erat is understood as the predicate, and the same verb must be supplied in four out of the five succeeding clauses, twice in the singular, with spēs (23) and senātus (23), and twice in the plural, with rēs (24) and ea (24). Cn. Pompēius: born in 106 B.C., consul in 70, Gnaeus Pompey was Rome's foremost military commander in this period. In 65, he was put in charge of the war in Asia Minor against the foreign monarch Mithridates, and he did not return to Rome until late 62.

23 ipsī: i.e., Catiline (dative of possession). *cōnsulātus, -ūs (m), consulship. nihil: = nōn, to be taken closely with the adjective intentus, -a, -um ("on the watch," "vigilant"). sānē, at all, by any means, very.

24 ea: neuter plural; i.e., the conditions in Italy and abroad that have just been enumerated. prōrsus, thoroughly, in every respect.

26 *nī: = nisi. spectāta . . . forent: pluperfect passive subjunctive (forent = essent); although the two nouns forming the compound subject of this verb are feminine, since these words denote things rather than persons, the participle is put in the neuter plural. What kind of condition is conveyed by this tense of the subjunctive? mihi: dative of agent = ā mē. nēquīquam, to no purpose, in vain.

28 per ignāviam aut vāna ingenia: the abstract noun ignāvia, -ae (f), "cowardice," is substituted for the expression ignāvōs hominēs; likewise vāna ingenia stands for hominēs vānī ingenī (lit., "men of worthless [*vānus, -a, -um] character"). Translate "with the backing of (lit., through) cowardly and unreliable supporters." incertus, -a, -um, uncertain, unsettled. incerta: neuter accusative plural, direct object, "a risky course of action."

29 captō (1) (*frequentative of* capiō), to grasp at, aim at, go in for (a course of action). What force is given to this clause by putting the verb in the imperfect subjunctive rather than the pluperfect? *quia, because. tempestātibus: "critical situations." What use of the ablative?

30 fīdus, -a, -um: faithful. mihi: dative with the predicate adjective fīdōs after the verb cognōvī (29). eō (adv.): = ideō, for that reason, consequently. animus: supply meus; animus meus virtually = ego. pulcher, pulchra, pulchrum, beautiful, (here figurative) fine, glorious.

31 vōbīs: dative of possession in the indirect statement eadem (neuter accusative plural) . . . esse.

14

15 Agitābātur magis magisque in diēs animus ferōx inopiā reī familiāris et
cōnscientiā scelerum, quae utraque eīs artibus auxerat quās suprā
memorāvī. Incitābant praetereā corruptī cīvitātis mōrēs, quōs pessuma ac
dīvorsa inter sē mala, lūxuria atque avāritia, vexābant.

*Various conditions favored Catiline's schemes. Many people faced finan-
cial ruin as a result of their debts; this group included many of the ex-
soldiers who had fought under the Roman general and dictator Sulla, and
they longed for a return to the days of pillage and turmoil. Rome's foremost military commander, Pompey, and the better part of her legions
were engaged in a war overseas and posed no threat to the success of the
conspirators' plan for an armed rebellion.*

[16.] Catilīna, simul quod aes aliēnum per omnīs terrās ingēns erat, et
20 quod plērīque Sullānī mīlitēs, largius suō ūsī, rapīnārum et victōriae
veteris memorēs, cīvīle bellum exoptābant, opprimundae reī pūblicae
cōnsilium cēpit. In Italiā nūllus exercitus; Cn. Pompēius in extrēmīs terrīs
bellum gerēbat; ipsī cōnsulātum petentī magna spēs; senātus nihil sānē
intentus; tūtae tranquillaeque rēs omnēs; sed ea prōrsus opportūna
25 Catilīnae.

*Catiline a candidate for the consulship in 64 B.C., calls a secret meeting
of his most loyal supporters shortly before the midsummer elections.
Many Roman senators and important citizens attend this meeting, which
takes place, according to Sallust, about the first of June. Catiline urges
his followers to join with him in seizing wealth and power from those
currently in control of the state. Because he has confidence in the courage
and dedication of his supporters, Catiline is hopeful that his scheme to
gain control of the government will succeed.*

[20.] "Nī virtūs fidēsque vostra satis spectāta mihi forent, nēquīquam
opportūna rēs cecidisset; spēs magna, dominātiō in manibus frūstrā
fuissent, neque ego per ignāviam aut vāna ingenia incerta prō certīs
captārem. Sed quia multīs et magnīs tempestātibus vōs cognōvī fortīs
30 fidōsque mihi, eō animus ausus est maxumum atque pulcherrumum
facinus incipere, simul quia vōbīs eadem quae mihi bona malaque esse
intellēxī; nam idem velle atque idem nōlle, ea dēmum firma amīcitia est.

1. **What two factors especially drove Catiline to desperate means?** (15–16)
2. **What was the moral climate in Rome at the time of the conspiracy?** (17–18)
3. **Why were conditions in Italy favorable to Catiline?** (19–22)
4. **Did Pompey or the Roman Senate threaten the success of the conspiracy?** (22–24)
5. **What qualities in his supporters encouraged Catiline to adopt a risky course of action?** (26–30)
6. **How does Catiline define the term** *amīcitia?* (32)

---

32 **ea**: the demonstrative pronoun gathers up the infinitives **velle** and **nōlle**, which
with their objects **idem . . . idem** supply the grammatical subject of **est. Ea** is
attracted into the feminine by the gender of the predicate nominative **amīcitia.**
dēmum, indeed. Emphasizes the demonstrative **ea.**

33 **quae . . . agitāvī**: "the projects that I have pondered." **dīvorsī**: agreeing with the subject of **audīstis** (= **audīvistis**); translate as an adverb, "separately." * **cēterum** (*adv.*), yet.

34 ***accendō, accendere** (3), **accendī, accēnsum**, to set on fire, inflame, excite. ***cōnsīderō** (1), to contemplate, consider. **cum cōnsīderō quae condiciō**: the *alliteration* of *c*, begun earlier in **Cēterum . . . accenditur**, adds force and brings out the bitterness of these words.

35 **futūra sit**: what use of the subjunctive? **nōsmet**: accusative plural, intensive of **nōs**. **vindicō** (1), to lay (legal) claim to. **vindicāmus in lībertātem**: an idiom meaning "set free."

36 **paucōrum potentium**: Catiline refers to the narrow circle of aristocrats within the Senate, the self-styled **optimātēs**, who exercised great influence over the conduct of public affairs. ***iūs, iūris** (*n*), right, justice, jurisdiction. **diciō, diciōnis** (*f*), dominion, power, control. **illīs**: i.e., the **paucī potentēs**, dative with the predicate adjective **vectīgālēs** (37) and also with **stīpendia pendere** (37). The infinitives **esse** and **pendere** are historical, equivalent to the imperfect indicative, and each has two nominatives as its subjects.

37 **tetrarchēs, -ae** (*m*) (*Greek loan word*), ruler of the quarter part of a larger kingdom, petty monarch. **vectīgālis, -is, -e**, tributary, paying tribute.

38 ***strēnuus, -a, -um**, active, energetic. **ignōbilis, -is, -e**, of humble birth. **volgus**: = **vulgus**; the substitution of *o* for *u* after the consonant *v* is a deliberate archaism on Sallust's part; this older spelling will also be seen in such words as **novos** (68) = **novus**, and **voltū** (166).

39 **eīs**: dative with the adjective ***obnoxius, -a, -um**, "submissive." **formīdō, formīdinis** (*f*), fear, dread. What use of the dative and what construction do you observe here in combination with **quibus**?

40 ***itaque** (*adv.*), accordingly. **potentia, -ae** (*f*), power, influence (of the personal kind, rather than official or legal). **honōs**: an older spelling of the nominative **honor**. ***dīvitiae, -ārum** (*f pl*), wealth, riches.

41 **ubi**: = **apud quōs**. **repulsa, -ae** (*f*), defeat at the polls (in an election). **perīcula**: here in the sense of threats of prosecution and conviction in the courts. ***iūdicium, -ī** (*n*), trial, prosecution. **egestās, egestātis** (*f*), poverty, slender means.

42 ***quō ūsque . . . ?**, to what extent . . . ? how long . . . ?—here emphasized by ***tandem**, translate freely: "I ask you." These three words provide a vivid echo of the opening words of Cicero's first speech against Catiline (106). **ēmorior, ēmorī** (3), **ēmortuus sum**, to die. The infinitive supplies the grammatical subject of **praestat** (43) ("it is preferable, better"). **per virtūtem**: equivalent to an adverb or ablative of manner, "heroically"; likewise, **per dēdecus** (44).

43 **inhonestus, -a, -um**, inglorious, shameful. **ubi**: = **in quā**, here introducing a relative clause of characteristic, hence the subjunctive of the indefinite 2nd person singular, "the sort of life in which you have been. . . ." **aliēnae**: here with the meaning "someone else's." ***superbia, -ae** (*f*), haughtiness.

44 **lūdibrium, -ī** (*n*), object of contempt, plaything. **dēdecus, dēdecoris** (*n*), disgrace, dishonor. **enim vērō**, to be sure (strengthening ***vērum**, "but"). **prō . . . !** (*interjection*), oh . . . !, ah . . . ! Construe with the accusative of exclamation **fidem** (45). **deum**: the usual spelling of the genitive plural (= **deōrum**) when construed with **fidem**.

45 **vigeō, vigēre** (2), to be vigorous, active. **Viget . . . valet**: the chiasmus here (compare note on line 10) is made more striking by the alliteration of the corresponding words in each pair.

46 **contrā** (*adv.*), by contrast, conversely. **cōnsenēscō, cōnsenēscere** (3), **cōnsenuī**, to grow old, decline. The ablatives **annīs** and **dīvitiīs** are causal. ***tantum modo**, only, merely.

47 **inceptō**: the perfect participle in the ablative with **opus est** is best translated as a noun, "a beginning."

48 **quīn . . . ?**, why not . . . ? **Quīn** with the indicative, here of the verb **expergīscor, expergīscī** (3), **experrectus sum**, "to wake up," "rouse oneself," makes the question equivalent to a command or exhortation. **ēn**, behold! **illa, illa**: repeated for emphasis and agreeing with **lībertās**, the postponed antecedent of **quam**. By means of the demonstrative **illa**, Catiline indicates that he is using **lībertās** in a particular sense that is well known to his audience from their previous discussions of the need to change the status quo. **optō** (1), to desire, wish for. **optāstis**: = **optāvistis**.

16

Those currently in power hold such a monopoly of riches and influence that the only course of action left is a bold assault against this establishment, unless Catiline's listeners are prepared to remain virtual slaves.

"Sed ego quae mente agitāvī omnēs iam anteā dīvorsī audīstis. Cēterum mihi in diēs magis animus accenditur, cum cōnsīderō quae condiciō vītae
35 futūra sit, nisi nōsmet ipsī vindicāmus in lībertātem. Nam postquam rēs pūblica in paucōrum potentium iūs atque diciōnem concessit, semper illīs rēgēs, tetrarchae vectīgālēs esse, populī, nātiōnēs stīpendia pendere; cēterī omnēs, strēnuī, bonī, nōbilēs atque ignōbilēs, volgus fuimus sine grātiā, sine auctōritāte, eīs obnoxiī quibus, sī rēs pūblica valēret, formīdinī
40 essēmus. Itaque omnis grātia, potentia, honōs, dīvitiae apud illōs sunt aut ubi illī volunt; nōbīs relīquēre repulsās, perīcula, iūdicia, egestātem. Quae quō ūsque tandem patiēminī, ō fortissumī virī? Nōnne ēmorī per virtūtem praestat quam vītam miseram atque inhonestam, ubi aliēnae superbiae lūdibriō fueris, per dēdecus āmittere? Vērum enim vērō, prō deum atque
45 hominum fidem, victōria in manū nōbīs est. Viget aetās, animus valet; contrā illīs annīs atque dīvitiīs omnia cōnsenuērunt. Tantum modo inceptō opus est; cētera rēs expediet.

The rewards for success will be great. Conditions are favorable. Catiline will not fail to do his part, if the rest are willing to do theirs.

"Quīn igitur expergīsciminī? Ēn illa, illa quam saepe optāstis, lībertās, praetereā dīvitiae, decus, glōria in oculīs sita sunt; fortūna omnia ea
50 victōribus praemia posuit. Rēs, tempus, perīcula, egestās, bellī spolia magnifica magis quam ōrātiō mea vōs hortantur. Vel imperātōre vel mīlite mē ūtiminī; neque animus neque corpus ā vōbīs aberit. Haec ipsa, ut spērō, vōbīscum ūnā cōnsul agam, nisi forte mē animus fallit et vōs servīre magis quam imperāre parātī estis."

1. What current state of affairs does Catiline find most objectionable and a limitation on the *lībertās* of himself and his followers? (35–41)
2. Why should Catiline and his men expect to triumph easily over their opponents? (45–46)
3. If Catiline and his men have their way, how will political and economic conditions in Rome be altered? (48–51)
4. What role does Catiline offer to play in the revolution? (51–52)
5. What further aspects of Catiline's character are revealed by this speech? What themes seem out of place in a speech delivered by a candidate who is confident of being elected consul for the following year?

---

49 **decus, decoris** (*n*), honor, glory. **situs, -a, -um**, placed, situated.
50 **spolium, -ī** (*n*), spoil, plunder.
51 **magnificus, -a, -um**, grand, splendid. ***imperātor, imperātōris** (*m*), commander, general. This word and **mīlite** are to be taken in the predicate after **mē** (52). What word governs these ablatives?
52 ***absum, abesse** (*irreg.*), **āfuī, āfutūrus**, to be wanting (with **ā** + ablative)
54 **serviō** (4), to be a slave, be subservient.

55 **Q. Curius**: at this time no longer a senator (lines 56–57), Quintus Curius no doubt belonged to that class of debtors and ruined politicians who hoped to recover their standing if Catiline's plot succeeded. He later turned informer and is credited with saving Cicero's life from a plot to assassinate him in 63. ***haud**, not, by no means. **obscūrus, -a, -um**, dark, obscure, humble. **haud obscūrō locō**: ablative of source with **nātus**. The *litotes* **haud obscūrō** approaches the meaning of **summō**.

56 **flāgitium, -ī** (*n*), shameful act, crime, vice. **cooperiō, cooperīre** (4), **cooperuī, coopertum**, to cover over, overwhelm. **cēnsor, cēnsōris** (*m*), one of two Roman magistrates, elected normally every five years for a term of eighteen months to take the census and revise the roll of the Senate. **probrum, -ī** (*n*), disgrace, disgraceful conduct. **probrī grātiā**: = **propter probrum**.

57 **vānitās, vānitātis** (*f*), folly, lack of judgment. **īnsum, inesse** (*irreg.*), **īnfuī** (+ *dat.*), to be present in. ***audācia, -ae** (*f*), boldness, recklessness.

58 **reticeō, reticēre** (2), **reticuī**, to be silent about. **suamet**: the suffix **-met** intensifies the possessive adjective **suus, -a, -um**. **prōrsus**, in short.

59 **dīcere . . . facere**: these infinitives are here used as verbal nouns supplying the object of **habēbat** ("considered"). Translate freely, "he had no regard for what he said or did." **Fulviā**: nothing beyond what Sallust tells us is known about this mistress of Curius.

60 **stuprī vetus cōnsuētūdō**: "a long-standing love affair"; the word **stuprum, -ī** (*n*), "debauchery," "immorality," is used to categorize their intimacy as shameful and illicit, no doubt because Fulvia belonged to a prominent family, yet failed to observe the moral restraint that was expected of women belonging to the upper class. **cui**: the relative pronoun is here coordinating, standing for **sed eī** (i.e., **Fulviae**). The dative is to be construed with the adjective **grātus** as well as the verbs **largīrī** (61), **pollicērī** (61), and **minārī** (62). **inopiā**: ablative of cause.

61 **largior, largīrī** (4), **largītus sum**, to give lavishly, give lavish presents. **glōrior, glōriārī** (1), **glōriātus sum**, to boast. **maria montīsque**: i.e., he made lavish promises, as we say "to promise heaven and earth." This is *hyperbole*.

62 **minor, minārī** (1), **minātus sum** (+ *dat.* of person), to threaten. **interdum**, sometimes, occasionally. **ferrō**: lit., "with a sword" (ablative of means), i.e., he threatened her physically. **foret**: equivalent to **futūra esset**. By using the subjunctive and the reflexive pronoun **sibi** referring to the subject (Curius) of **coepit**, the author reports the words originally uttered by Curius in virtual indirect discourse. **Sibi** represents **mihi** of direct address, and **foret** replaces **eris**. ***postrēmō**, finally, in short. This adverb is used frequently by Sallust to introduce the last member of a series or to mark a climax. **agitāre**: "he behaved"; the infinitive is best taken as historical rather than complementary with **coepit** (61).

63 ***soleō, solēre** (2), **solitus sum**, to be accustomed. **insolentia, -ae** (*f*), lack of moderation, arrogance, unusual conduct. ***tālis, -is, -e**, such, of such a kind.

64 **dē Catilīnae coniūrātiōne**: logically this prepositional phrase belongs in the relative clause.

65 **quōque modō**: = **et quō modō**, i.e., Fulvia revealed in general terms, but without specifically naming her source (**sublātō auctōre**, 64), how she had learned of the plot from one of the conspirators.

66 ***studium, -ī** (*n*), zeal, eagerness, inclination.

67 **nōbilitās, nōbilitātis** (*f*), nobility, the nobles. Since this noun is used in a collective sense, it admits both a singular (**aestuābat**) and plural (**crēdēbant**, 68) predicate. ***invidia, -ae** (*f*), envy, jealousy. **aestuō** (1), to boil, seethe. ***quasi**, as if, as it were, almost.

68 **polluō, polluere** (3), **polluī, pollūtum**, to make foul, degrade, sully. **quamvīs** (*adv.*), however, no matter how. Construe with the adjective **ēgregius**. **homō novos**: usually written **novos** (= **novus**) **homō**, a technical term for an individual who was the first in his family to become a senator (in this period by being elected quaestor) and applied in a narrower sense to those who were the first in their families to be elected consul and hence to confer **nōbilitās** on their descendants.

69 ***adipīscor, adipīscī** (3), **adeptus sum**, to obtain, attain, secure. This verb is in the subjunctive because the **sī** clause is part of the indirect statement depending on **crēdēbant** (68). **adveniō, advenīre** (4), **advēnī, adventum**, to arrive, arise, develop. **post fuēre**: "were put aside"; the adverb **post** (lit., "behind in importance," "secondary") is used in place of a predicate adjective after **fuēre**.

One of the members of the conspiracy, an ex-senator named Quintus Curius, reveals to his mistress Fulvia the existence of Catiline's plot. Fulvia spreads news of this conspiracy, and the fear aroused in the populace adds support to the candidacy of Cicero, who was opposing Catiline in the consular elections.

55 **[23.]** Sed in eā coniūrātiōne fuit Q. Curius, nātus haud obscūrō locō, flāgitiīs atque facinoribus coopertus, quem cēnsōrēs senātū probrī grātiā mōverant. Huic hominī nōn minor vānitās inerat quam audācia; neque reticēre quae audierat, neque suamet ipse scelera occultāre, prōrsus neque dīcere neque facere quicquam pēnsī habēbat. Erat eī cum Fulviā, muliere
60 nōbilī, stuprī vetus cōnsuētūdō; cui cum minus grātus esset quia inopiā minus largīrī poterat, repente glōriāns, maria montīsque pollicērī coepit, et minārī interdum ferrō, nī sibi obnoxia foret; postrēmō ferōcius agitāre quam solitus erat. At Fulvia, insolentiae Curī causā cognitā, tāle perīculum reī pūblicae haud occultum habuit, sed sublātō auctōre dē Catilīnae
65 coniūrātiōne quae quōque modō audierat complūribus nārrāvit. Ea rēs in prīmīs studia hominum accendit ad cōnsulātum mandandum M. Tulliō Cicerōnī. Namque anteā plēraque nōbilitās invidiā aestuābat, et quasi polluī cōnsulātum crēdēbant, sī eum quamvīs ēgregius homō novos adeptus foret. Sed ubi perīculum advēnit, invidia atque superbia post fuēre.

1. **What factors may have induced Curius to join the conspiracy?** (55–63)
2. **Why did Fulvia not conceal what she had learned about the conspiracy?** (63–65)
3. **What disadvantage did Cicero have to overcome in seeking election to the consulship?** (67–69)

Bust of Cicero (?); identification not certain. Chiaramonti Museum, the Vatican

19

70 **comitia, -ōrum** (*n*), an assembly (of the people for voting), an election. ***dēclārō** (1), to declare, announce (as elected). **C. Antōnius**: allegedly an accomplice of Catiline, Gaius Antonius had been removed from the Senate by the censors in 70 B.C. for misconduct and regained his seat by holding the praetorship with Cicero in 66.

71 **quod factum**: **factum** is best regarded as a noun standing in apposition to the preceding statement taken as a whole and as supplying the antecedent of the coordinating relative **quod**. Translate freely: "and this outcome." **prīmō**, at first. ***populāris, populāris** (*m/f*), associate, accomplice. **concutiō, concutere** (3), **concussī, concussum**, to shake, distress, confound.

72 ***furor, furōris** (*m*), madness, frenzy. **agitō** (1), to plot, devise, set in motion. **agitāre**: the subject of this and the following historical infinitive is **Catilīna** (understood after **Catilīnae furor**).

73 **locīs opportūnīs**: a simple ablative denoting place where without the preposition **in**, common with the noun **locus** when it is modified by an adjective.

74 **mūtuus, -a, -um**, on loan. **sūmptam mūtuam**: "taken up on loan," "borrowed." **Faesulae, -ārum** (*f pl*), a town in Etruria near modern Florence (see map, p. 3). Land had been allotted to Sulla's veterans in this region, and it was a breeding ground for discontent thanks to the dispossessed landowners who had been displaced by the new settlers and the ex-soldiers of Sulla who had squandered their bounties. **Mānlium**: according to other sources, Gaius Manlius had served as a centurion under Sulla and so was an experienced military man.

76 ***conparō** (1), to prepare, provide. **nihilō minus** (*sometimes written as one word*), nonetheless. This expression indicates that the nature of the preceding ablative absolute is concessive. **proxumus, -a, -um**, next, following. I.e., for the year 62, at the elections in 63.

77 ***dēsignō** (1), to appoint, elect (to a magistracy). The pluperfect subjunctive is employed in this subordinate clause within an indirect statement to represent the future perfect indicative of direct discourse. ***facile** (*adv.*), easily. Construe with the infinitive **ūsūrum (esse)** (78). **ex voluntāte**: "according to his (i.e., Catiline's) wishes." Antonius had formed a coalition with Catiline to oppose Cicero for the consulship in 64; as consul in 63, Antonius remained a potential ally of Catiline within the government if conditions proved favorable. Cicero took great pains to detach Antonius from his former associate (see lines 82–83).

78 **ūsūrum**: supply **esse** to complete this future active infinitive in indirect discourse. What case does **ūtor** govern?

79 ***caveō, cavēre** (2), **cāvī, cautum**, to be on one's guard, take precautions. **dolus, -ī** (*m*), artifice, craft. **astūtia, -ae** (*f*), cunning, craft. The plural here suggests the sense "cunning methods." This word and the word **dolus** give a less than flattering description of Cicero's astuteness.

80 **prīncipium, -ī** (*n*), beginning.

81 ***paulō**: ablative of degree of difference with the adverb **ante**, lit., "by a little." The reference is to lines 55–63. **sibi**: i.e., Cicero, the subject of **effēcerat**, since the **ut** clause states not only a result but also expresses the intention of the subject of the leading verb.

82 **Ad hoc**: "in addition to this," i.e., the recruitment of Curius as an informer through Fulvia. **pactiō, pactiōnis** (*f*), agreement, compact (+ objective genitive). Cicero secured Antonius' cooperation in his efforts to combat Catiline's schemes by exchanging with his colleague the provinces that had been assigned to them to govern as proconsuls in the following year. By this arrangement, Antonius swapped Cisalpine Gaul for Macedonia, which offered better prospects for winning military glory and gaining riches. **perpellō, perpellere** (3), **perpulī, perpulsum**, to prevail on, constrain.

83 **sentiō, sentīre** (4), **sēnsī, sēnsum**, to entertain a particular attitude (especially with reference to patriotism or loyalty).

84 **Catilīnae**, dative of reference (advantage) with **prōsperē cessēre** (85–86, "turned out successfully").

85 **petītiō, petītiōnis** (*f*), candidacy. **campō**: the Campus Martius ("Plain of Mars"), an open area outside the city walls to the northwest of the Capitoline Hill and bounded by a bend in the Tiber River. This was the customary place for holding elections since the **comitia centuriāta**, the assembly that elected praetors and consuls, because of its military character, could not be convened within the sacred boundary (**pōmērium**) of the city.

Following his failure to be elected consul in 64, Catiline went ahead with plans to gather arms and money to further the cause of armed revolution.

70 **[24.]** Igitur comitiīs habitīs, cōnsulēs dēclārantur M. Tullius et C. Antōnius; quod factum prīmō populārīs coniūrātiōnis concusserat. Neque tamen Catilīnae furor minuēbātur, sed in diēs plūra agitāre, arma per Italiam locīs opportūnīs parāre, pecūniam suā aut amīcōrum fidē sūmptam mūtuam Faesulās ad Mānlium quendam portāre, quī posteā prīnceps fuit
75 bellī faciundī.

In 63 Cicero is kept informed of Catiline's secret plans by Curius, who agreed to act as a spy. Catiline fails once more to be elected consul and decides to have recourse to open insurrection.

[26.] Hīs rēbus conparātīs, Catilīna nihilō minus in proxumum annum cōnsulātum petēbat, spērāns sī dēsignātus foret, facile sē ex voluntāte Antōniō ūsūrum. Neque intereā quiētus erat, sed omnibus modīs īnsidiās parābat Cicerōnī. Neque illī tamen ad cavendum dolus aut astūtiae
80 dēerant. Namque ā prīncipiō cōnsulātūs suī multa pollicendō per Fulviam effēcerat ut Q. Curius, dē quō paulō ante memorāvī, cōnsilia Catilīnae sibi prōderet. Ad hoc collēgam suum Antōnium pactiōne prōvinciae perpulerat nē contrā rem pūblicam sentīret; circum sē praesidia amīcōrum atque clientium occultē habēbat. Postquam diēs comitiōrum vēnit, et Catilīnae
85 neque petītiō neque īnsidiae quās cōnsulibus in campō fēcerat prōsperē cessēre, cōnstituit bellum facere et extrēma omnia experīrī, quoniam quae occultē temptāverat aspera foedaque ēvēnerant.

1. How could the election of Antonius be viewed as a partial success by the conspirators? (See note on line 77.)
2. How did Catiline's supporters react to his defeat in the consular elections in 64? (71)
3. How did Catiline raise money to further his schemes? (73–74)
4. Why was the town of Faesulae selected as a headquarters? (See note on line 74.)
5. How did Cicero neutralize the threat posed by his colleague Antonius? (82–83)
6. Why was Catiline driven to desperation by his defeat in the elections in 63? (85–87 and Introduction, p. 4)

---

87 *asper, aspera, asperum, rough, hard, adverse. *foedus, -a, -um, foul, detestable, disastrous. *ēveniō, ēvenīre (4), ēvēnī, ēventum, to come forth, come to pass, turn out.

88 **C. Mānlium Faesulās**: Manlius had come to Rome with a band of men to support Catiline's candidacy and was now sent back to Faesulae after the elections, held probably at the usual time in midsummer.

89 **Septimium ... Camertem**: Septimius, a native of Camerinum, a town in eastern Umbria, and Gaius Iulius—not to be confused with the future dictator Gaius Iulius Caesar—-were agents of Catiline about whom little else is known. Presumably they had some influence at the local level in the regions of Picenum (bordering Umbria and facing the Adriatic, to the northeast of Rome) and Apulia (also facing the Adriatic, in the southeast of the Italian peninsula). See map, p. 2.

90 ***dīmittō, dīmittere** (3), **dīmīsī, dīmissum**, to send off, dispatch. **alium, aliō**: "others to various places," lit., "another to another place." The pronoun **alius** is here used in a distributive sense in combination with the cognate adverb **aliō**. The singular **alium** stands in partitive apposition to an understood plural object, such as **sociōs**, governed by **dīmīsit** to be supplied from the previous clause. **quem ... crēdēbat**: "wherever (**ubīque**, lit., 'anywhere') he thought that each would be (**fore** = **futūrum esse**) advantageous to him."

91 ***mōlior, mōlīrī** (4), **mōlītus sum**, to attempt, undertake, contrive. **Mōlīrī** is the first in a series of ten historical infinitives in *asyndeton* (i.e., the conjunctions are omitted) to convey a frenzy of activity. Supply **Catilīna** as the subject. **tendō, tendere** (3), **tetendī, tentum**, to stretch, (with **īnsidiās**, "plots") to lay.

92 ***incendium, -ī** (*n*), fire, conflagration. **armātīs**: "armed," modifying **hominibus**, an instrumental ablative rather than agent because the ablative states the means by which Catiline achieved his goal. **cum tēlō esse**: a stock expression meaning "he was armed."

93 **item**: supply **cum tēlō esse**, the infinitive being governed by **iubēre**. **aliōs**: = **cēterōs**. **utī**: = **ut**, introducing the indirect command after **hortārī**. **diēs noctīsque**: what use of the accusative?

94 ***festīnō** (1), to hasten, be active. This verb is sometimes, as here, used to convey a flurry of activity that accomplishes little. **vigilō** (1), to be awake, go without sleep. **īnsomnium, -ī** (*n*) (*usually pl*), sleeplessness. **fatīgō** (1), to tire out, weary, exhaust.

95 **Quibus rēbus**: = **Et eīs rēbus**, i.e., the activities of Catiline and his associates as well as the countermeasures taken by the government (described in a chapter not included in this reader). **permoveō, permovēre** (2), **permōvī, permōtum**, to stir violently, alarm, agitate. **inmūtō** (1), to alter, change in form. ***faciēs, -ēī** (*f*), form, appearance, face. **urbis faciēs**: "the outward appearance of the city."

96 **laetitia, -ae** (*f*), joy, gladness, (here) unrestrained joyfulness and its external manifestations. **lascīvia, -ae** (*f*), unruly behavior, wantonness. **diūturna quiēs**: since Sulla's victory in the civil war in 82, the city of Rome had enjoyed relative peace; hence the description of this period of tranquillity as "long-continued" (**diūturnus, -a, -um**). **pariō, parere** (3), **peperī, partum**, to produce, bring about.

97 **trīstitia, -ae** (*f*), sadness, gloom. **festīnāre**: the first in a series of six historical infinitives in asyndeton (compare note on line 91) intended to convey panic and disarray. **Omnēs** is easily understood as subject after **omnis**, the accusative direct object of **invāsit**. **trepidō** (1), to be in a state of panic, be anxious. **cuiquam**: used adjectivally (= **ūllī**), with the two dative objects of **crēdere** (98).

98 **neque bellum ... habēre**: "were not engaged in a full state of war, yet lacked peace." **suō ... metū**: ablative of the standard of measure with **mētīrī** (99).

100 **tametsī**, although, though.

101 **lēge Plautiā**: the ablative denotes the law under which Catiline was indicted; the **lēx Plautia** covered acts of violence (**vīs**) against the state as well as against individuals. This is the statute under which members of the conspiracy were tried in 62 B.C. ***interrogō** (1), to inquire, examine, indict. **L. Paulō**: consul in 50 B.C. and son of the consul in 78 who raised a revolt, Lucius Aemilius Lepidus Paulus was the brother of the future triumvir who shared power with Antony and Octavian in 43 B.C.

102 ***dissimulō** (1), to conceal, hide, feign ignorance. **expurgō** (1), to clear from blame, justify. **iūrgium, -ī** (*n*), abuse, vituperation. **lacessītus foret**: pluperfect subjunctive in secondary sequence after **sīcut** ("just as if"), introducing a conditional clause of comparison (here, past contrary to fact). **in senātum vēnit**: the meeting can be dated to 8 November. On the morning of the day before, two of Catiline's henchmen tried to assassinate Cicero in his home, but Cicero had been warned of this plot by the spy Curius in time to take precautions.

*Catiline dispatches Manlius and other followers to organize rebellion in
various regions of Italy. In Rome, he lays plans to murder the consuls, set
fires in the city to cause panic on the night of the uprising, and seize
strategic points with armed men.*

[27.] Igitur C. Mānlium Faesulās atque in eam partem Etrūriae,
Septimium quendam Camertem in agrum Pīcēnum, C. Iūlium in Apūliam
90 dīmīsit; praetereā alium aliō, quem ubīque opportūnum sibi fore crēdēbat.
Intereā Rōmae multa simul mōlīrī, cōnsulibus īnsidiās tendere, parāre
incendia, opportūna loca armātīs hominibus obsidēre, ipse cum tēlō esse,
item aliōs iubēre, hortārī utī semper intentī parātīque essent, diēs
noctīsque festīnāre, vigilāre, neque īnsomniīs neque labōre fatīgārī.

*Catiline's activities throw the city of Rome into a state of panic. Al-
though indicted on criminal charges, he is not deterred but continues to
plot revolution in secret and plays the part of an innocent citizen slan-
dered by false accusations. When he attends a meeting of the Senate in
early November, 63 B.C., Cicero takes Catiline to task for his duplicity.*

95 [31a.] Quibus rēbus permōta cīvitās atque inmūtāta urbis faciēs erat. Ex
summā laetitiā atque lascīviā, quae diūturna quiēs pepererat, repente
omnīs trīstitia invāsit; festīnāre, trepidāre, neque locō nec hominī cuiquam
satis crēdere, neque bellum gerere neque pācem habēre, suō quisque metū
perīcula mētīrī.
100 At Catilīnae crūdēlis animus eadem illa movēbat, tametsī praesidia
parābantur et ipse lēge Plautiā interrogātus erat ab L. Paulō. Postrēmō,
dissimulandī causā aut suī expurgandī, sīcut iūrgiō lacessītus foret, in
senātum vēnit. Tum M. Tullius cōnsul, sīve praesentiam eius timēns, sīve
īrā commōtus, ōrātiōnem habuit lūculentam atque ūtilem reī pūblicae,
105 quam posteā scrīptam ēdidit.

1. **What instructions did Catiline give to his supporters?** (93)
2. **Why was arson such a threat to the safety of all in the city of Rome?**
3. **What action was taken by Lucius Paulus to curb Catiline's activities?** (101)
4. **How did Cicero react to the presence of Catiline in the Senate?** (103–104)
5. **How can we explain Sallust's decision not to present a version of Cicero's *First
   Catilinarian* as part of his history of the conspiracy?** (105)

---

103 **praesentia, -ae** (*f*), presence.
104 **commoveō, commovēre** (2), **commōvī, commōtum**, to move violently, excite.
   lūculentus, -a, -um, splendid, fine, brilliant. **reī pūblicae**: what word governs this
   dative?
105 **ēdō, ēdere** (3), **ēdidī, ēditum**, to put forth, publish.

106 **Quō ūsque tandem**: compare Catiline's use of this phrase to denote his impatience (42). **abūtor, abūtī** (3), **abūsus sum** (+ *abl.*), to exhaust by using, take (unscrupulous) advantage of. **abūtēre**: **-re** is the spelling Cicero preferred for the 2nd person singular when a deponent verb, or verb in the passive voice, is future (compare **interficiēre**, 139); **-ris** is the normal spelling in the present tense (e.g., **arbitrāris**, 114). **patientia, -ae** (*f*), patience, forbearance.

107 **ēlūdō, ēlūdere** (3), **ēlūsī, ēlūsum**, to mock, flout. **effrēnātus, -a, -um**, unrestrained, violent. **iactō** (1) (+ *the reflexive* **sēsē**), to flaunt oneself, swagger.

108 **Nihilne**: **nihil**, repeated six times for emphasis (*anaphora*) with each successive subject, is adverbial, = **nōn**; lit., "in no respect," "not at all." **nocturnus, -a, -um**, occurring at night, nocturnal. **Palātī**: the Palatine, one of the seven hills of Rome, was a fashionable quarter in which many wealthy senators had their homes (see plan, p. 5). The garrison by night was intended to protect the lives and property of these key government figures from Catiline's plots. ***vigiliae, -ārum** (*f pl*), guards, patrols, watches. When in late October the Senate began to adopt countermeasures in response to the threat posed by the activities of the conspirators, these patrols were established throughout the city and assigned to the oversight of the lesser magistrates by a decree of the Senate.

109 ***timor, timōris** (*m*) fear. **concursus, -ūs** (*m*) a flocking together, assembly. **bonōrum**: "patriots" as opposed to wicked citizens (**improbī**) who favored the disruption of the state. Those who stood for the status quo and the influence of the Senate styled themselves the **optimātēs** (lit. "the best" class of citizens), while the term **bonī** is more inclusive and meant to embrace all citizens not in sympathy with the aims of the conspirators. **hic mūnītissimus . . . locus**: "this most fortified place for (lit., of) holding a meeting of the Senate." The Senate was convened on this occasion in the Temple of Jupiter Stator situated at the foot of the Palatine Hill, near the **via Sacra** (see plan, p. 6). It is called **mūnītissimus** because the temple had been surrounded by an armed guard of loyal citizens drawn especially from the equestrian class (i.e., citizens who belonged to the highest census classification but had not held public office).

110 **ōra vultūsque**: the faces (**ōs, ōris**, *n*) and facial expressions (***vultus, -ūs**, *m*) of the senators present at this meeting registered their fear and loathing of Catiline.

111 **cōnstringō, cōnstringere** (3), **cōnstrīnxī, cōnstrictum**, to restrain, inhibit. The participle is to be taken as a predicate adjective after the infinitive **tenērī** in indirect discourse introduced by **vidēs** (112).

112 **Quid . . . ēgeris**: "What you did last night (**proximus, -a, -um**, lit., 'nearest,' 'immediately preceding') and what you did the night before last," the first in a series of indirect questions supplying the object of the infinitive **ignōrāre** (113) in indirect discourse. The words **superiōre nocte** allude to a meeting of the conspirators on the night of 6/7 November when they formed a plan to assassinate Cicero in his home on the following morning.

113 ***convocō** (1), to summon together, assemble. **cōnsilī**: what use of the genitive with **quid**? **quem nostrum**: "which one of us"; the accusative **quem** supplies the subject of the infinitive **ignōrāre**. **Nostrum** is a partitive genitive.

115 **Ō tempora, ō mōrēs!**: accusative of exclamation, "What times (are these), what conduct (is this)!"

116 **immō**, on the contrary, (+ **vērō**) why!

117 **particeps, participis** (*m/f*), sharer, participant in. Construe with the objective genitive **pūblicī cōnsilī** (116), "public debate." **notō** (1), to mark, single out. **dēsignō** (1), to indicate, point out. **ūnum quemque nostrum**: i.e., individual members of the Senate, such as Cicero, who posed the greatest obstacle to Catiline's schemes. The Senate was not unanimous in its opposition to the conspirators. A handful of senators and the praetor Lentulus actively participated in the conspiracy.

118 **fortēs virī**: this appositive to **nōs** is loaded with *irony*, given the lack of resolve to inflict punishment on Catiline. **reī pūblicae**: dative with **satis facere**, "to discharge one's (here, 'our') duty."

119 **vītēmus**: present subjunctive of the indefinite future "if we should go on avoiding . . . ." **iussū**, (+ *gen. or a possessive adjective*), at the command of. ***iam prīdem**, long ago, well before now.

120 **cōnferō, cōnferre** (*irreg.*), **contulī, collātum**, to bring together, apply, direct. With the infinitive, supply **oportēbat**. ***pestis, pestis** (*f*), plague, ruin, destruction. **māchinor, māchinārī** (1), **māchinātus sum**, to devise, contrive.

Cicero asks rhetorically how much longer Catiline hopes to indulge in his mad schemes. The consul outlines the provisions that have been made to block Catiline's plots, and he asserts that Catiline's intention to overthrow the government is no longer secret but known to all.

[1.] "Quō ūsque tandem abūtēre, Catilīna, patientiā nostrā? Quam diū etiam furor iste tuus nōs ēlūdet? Quem ad fīnem sēsē effrēnāta iactābit audācia? Nihilne tē nocturnum praesidium Palātī, nihil urbis vigiliae, nihil timor populī, nihil concursus bonōrum omnium, nihil hic mūnītissimus habendī senātūs locus, nihil hōrum ōra vultūsque mōvērunt? Patēre tua cōnsilia nōn sentīs? Cōnstrictam iam hōrum omnium scientiā tenērī coniūrātiōnem tuam nōn vidēs? Quid proximā, quid superiōre nocte ēgeris, ubi fuerīs, quōs convocāverīs, quid cōnsilī cēperīs, quem nostrum ignōrāre arbitrāris?

Cicero and the Senate have been far too lenient in failing to act against Catiline. In past generations, Roman citizens were put to death for threatening the security of the state. Catiline, who threatens the very existence of the state, not only has escaped punishment to date but continues to enjoy the status of a senator and to take part in public deliberations.

[2.] "Ō tempora, ō mōrēs! Senātus haec intellegit, cōnsul videt; hic tamen vīvit. Vīvit? Immō vērō etiam in senātum venit, fit pūblicī cōnsilī particeps, notat et dēsignat oculīs ad caedem ūnum quemque nostrum. Nōs autem, fortēs virī, satis facere reī pūblicae vidēmur, sī istīus furōrem ac tēla vītēmus. Ad mortem tē, Catilīna, dūcī iussū cōnsulis iam prīdem oportēbat; in tē cōnferrī pestem, quam tū in nōs māchināris.

1. **What measures had been taken by the government to ward off danger to the city?** (108–109)
2. **To what extent, according to Cicero, were Catiline's plans known to the senators?** (110–114)
3. **How are we to explain Catiline's decision to attend this meeting of the Senate?** (116–117)
4. **What punishment was deserved by Catiline according to Cicero?** (119–120)

121 **vir amplissimus**: the positive degree is usually appropriate for translating the superlative of adjectives of praise or blame modifying **vir** (or **homō**) standing in apposition to the name of a person. **P. Scīpiō**: Publius Cornelius Scipio Nasica, consul in 138 B.C., led the mob that attacked and killed the tribune Tiberius Gracchus and some of his supporters in 133 B.C., when Gracchus was seeking to have himself re-elected tribune for the following year. **pontifex, pontificis** (*m*), one of the college of priests who superintended matters of public religion in Rome; the head of this college was styled the **pontifex maximus**.

122 **mediocriter**: Gracchus had passed legislation over the opposition of the Senate and had used the popular assembly to challenge some of the Senate's prerogatives in managing foreign affairs and fiscal matters. Cicero's point is that the harm done to the state by Gracchus was relatively moderate in contrast with Catiline's plan to devastate the world (**orbem terrae**, 123) with fire and sword; yet the former had been put to death by Scipio, who held no public office at the time (**prīvātus**), while Catiline received no punishment at the hands of the chief magistrates (**nōs cōnsulēs perferēmus**, 123–124). **labefactō** (1), to weaken, undermine. **status, -ūs** (*m*), condition, public order.

123 **orbis, orbis** (*m*), circle. **orbis terrae** (*or* **terrārum**), the earth, the whole world.

124 **perferō, perferre** (*irreg.*), **pertulī, perlātum**, to tolerate, put up with. **quod**: "the fact that . . ."; the **quod** clause stands in apposition to **illa nimis antīqua** and gives an instance of what Cicero means by those precedents for dealing harshly with traitors that might be cited from remote antiquity. **C. Servīlius Ahāla Sp. Maelium**: the patrician Servilius Ahala, while serving as Master of the Horse under the dictator Cincinnatus in 439 B.C., is reported to have killed Maelius, a wealthy plebeian who had won great popularity among the common people by relieving a food shortage and so fell under the suspicion of aiming at tyranny (here described as "being eager for a revolution," **novīs rēbus studentem**, 125).

125 **Fuit**: repeated for emphasis, "there existed," a common meaning of the verb **sum** when it is the first word in a sentence.

126 **ista**: the usual implication of contempt is lacking to **ista** here (contrast line 107), and it is virtually equivalent to **illa**: "that well-known (of which you have heard)." **quondam**, once, once upon a time, formerly.

127 **perniciōsus, -a, -um**, destructive, ruinous. *****acerbus, -a, -um**, bitter, harsh, violent. **coerceō, coercēre** (2), **coercuī, coercitum**, to suppress, curb.

128 **senātūs cōnsultum**: a decree of the Senate, further described by the adjectives **vehemēns** and **grave**. Cicero refers to the so-called **senātūs cōnsultum ultimum**, passed in this instance on 21 October, which instructed the consuls to take all necessary steps to preserve the state from harm; it in effect suspended for the duration of the emergency all legal restrictions normally placed upon the authority of the chief magistrates.

129 **huius ōrdinis**: "of this body," i.e., the Roman Senate. **apertē**, openly, frankly.

130 **dēsumus**: supply the dative **reī pūblicae**.

131 **sunt**: construe with the participle **conlocāta** (132). **faucēs, faucium** (*f*), throat, jaws, pass, defile. **in Etrūriae faucibus**: Manlius' camp near the town of Faesulae was situated in the vicinity of a narrow pass leading through a western spur of the Apennine Mountains.

132 **crēscō, crēscere** (3), **crēvī, crētum**, to grow, increase. **in diēs singulōs**: "each successive day" (see the note on **in diēs**, line 15).

133 **imperātōrem ducemque**: i.e., Catiline. These two accusatives serve as the object of **vidēmus** (134) and are modified by the participle **mōlientem** (135), whose object is **perniciem** (134). *****moenia, moenium** (*n pl*), defensive walls, city walls. **adeō**, even, actually. This adverb adds emphasis to the phrase **in senātū**.

134 *****intestīnus, -a, -um**, internal. *****perniciēs, -ēī** (*f*), physical destruction, ruin.

135 *****comprehendō, comprehendere** (3), **comprehendī, comprehēnsum**, to seize, arrest. **crēdō**: spoken ironically since the clause of fearing expresses just the opposite of what Cicero claims to be likely to cause him concern.

136 **erit verendum mihi**: "I shall have to fear"; the grammatical subject of the passive periphrastic is supplied by the substantive **nē** clause of fearing. **nē nōn potius . . . quam**: "not so much that . . . but rather that. . . ." (lit., "not rather that . . . than that. . . ."). Supply from the second of the two clauses **factum esse dīcant** as the predicate of **omnēs**. **sērius**, too late, later than was proper or fitting.

137 **hoc**: i.e., the arrest and execution of Catiline. This neuter pronoun serves as the object of **faciam** (138) and the antecedent of **quod**.

[3.] "An vērō vir amplissimus P. Scīpiō, pontifex maximus, Ti. Gracchum, mediocriter labefactantem statum reī pūblicae, prīvātus interfēcit; Catilīnam, orbem terrae caede atque incendiīs vastāre cupientem, nōs cōnsulēs perferēmus? Nam illa nimis antīqua praetereō, quod C. Servīlius
125 Ahāla Sp. Maelium, novīs rēbus studentem, manū suā occīdit. Fuit, fuit ista quondam in hāc rē pūblicā virtūs, ut virī fortēs ācriōribus suppliciīs cīvem perniciōsum quam acerbissimum hostem coercērent. Habēmus senātūs cōnsultum in tē, Catilīna, vehemēns et grave; nōn dēest reī pūblicae cōnsilium neque auctōritās huius ōrdinis. Nōs, nōs, dīcō apertē,
130 cōnsulēs dēsumus.

If Cicero takes advantage of the emergency powers granted to him by decree of the Senate and orders the execution of Catiline, he is more likely to be criticized for his failure to act sooner than for the severity of his action. Yet Catiline's life will be spared so long as even a few are prepared to defend his conduct.

[5.] "Castra sunt in Italiā contrā populum Rōmānum in Etrūriae faucibus conlocāta, crēscit in diēs singulōs hostium numerus; eōrum autem castrōrum imperātōrem ducemque hostium intrā moenia atque adeō in senātū vidēmus intestīnam aliquam cōtīdiē perniciem reī pūblicae
135 mōlientem. Sī tē iam, Catilīna, comprehendī, sī interficī iusserō, crēdō, erit verendum mihi, nē nōn potius hoc omnēs bonī sērius ā mē quam quisquam crūdēlius factum esse dīcat. Vērum ego hoc, quod iam prīdem factum esse oportuit, certā dē causā nōndum addūcor ut faciam. Tum dēnique interficiēre, cum iam nēmō tam improbus, tam perditus, tam tuī
140 similis invenīrī poterit, quī id nōn iūre factum esse fateātur.

1. **What precedents are cited by Cicero for punishing traitors without due process of law? To what degree did Catiline pose a greater threat?** (121–125)
2. **How are the Romans of old said to have treated wicked citizens?** (126–127)
3. **What extraordinary power had been granted to the consuls by the Senate to meet the threat posed by the conspiracy? How are we to account for Cicero's reluctance to exercise this power?** (127–130)
4. **Why was it to Catiline's advantage to delay his departure from Rome? What could he hope to accomplish by remaining in Rome while his lieutenant Manlius looked after affairs at Faesulae?** (133–135)
5. **What conditions must prevail, according to Cicero, before he orders Catiline's execution?** (139–140)

---

138 **factum esse oportuit**: "ought to have been over and done with"; the perfect infinitive stresses the need for the completion of the act, while the present infinitive, which is ordinarily used with the past tense of **oportet**, would convey the simple notion of the obligation to perform a given act in the past. I.e., **hoc mē facere oportuit** = "I ought to have done this," while **hoc mē fēcisse oportuit** = "I ought to have finished doing this." *addūcō, addūcere (3), addūxī, adductum, to lead, induce (to adopt a certain course of action—expressed by **ut** + the subjunctive).
139 *dēnique, at last, finally. *perditus, -a, -um, ruined, reckless, abandoned.
140 **similis**: what case does the adjective **similis** take when the noun or pronoun denotes a person? **poterit**: the verb is in the indicative because the **cum** clause is strictly temporal in reference to the adverb **tum** (138) in the main clause. *iūre, rightfully, justly. *fateor, fatērī (2), fassus sum, to admit, confess, acknowledge. Why must the verb in this relative clause be put in the subjunctive?

141 **Quae cum**: = **et cum ea** ("these things," neuter). This is a very common use of the coordinating relative pronoun to introduce a **cum** causal clause to sum up after a series of facts has been enumerated. **pergō, pergere** (3), **perrēxī, perrēctum**, to make one's way, proceed. **quō coepistī: pergere** is understood, "whence you began (to make your way)." Catiline is portrayed as being on the verge of departing from Rome. It seems, in fact, that the date of his departure had been set at the meeting of the conspirators two nights previously (see note on line 112). It may be that the failure of the plot to assassinate Cicero on 7 November (see note on line 102) had caused Catiline to remain in Rome a day or two longer than planned. The principal object of Cicero's speech was to bring Catiline's guilt out into the open by causing him to leave Rome and join the army of Manlius in Etruria. So long as Catiline remained in Rome, public sentiment was likely to remain divided as to Catiline's guilt or innocence. *__**ēgredior, ēgredī**__ (3), **ēgressus sum**, to go out, leave. **aliquandō**, at some time, finally, now at last. Construe with the imperative **ēgredere**.

142 **nimium**, too. Construe with **diū**. **tua illa Mānliāna castra**: "that well-known camp of yours under the care of Manlius."

143 *__**ēdūcō, ēdūcere**__ (3), **ēdūxī, ēductum**, to lead out, lead forth. What are the other three verbs that drop the vowel termination of the imperative singular? **sī minus**: "failing that," lit., "if not" (**minus** = **nōn**), with **omnīs** (accusative) understood. The expression connects the two objects of **ēdūc: omnīs tuōs** and **quam plūrimōs** ("as many as possible").

144 **pūrgō** (1), to free from impurities, purify, cleanse. The implication is that Catiline's associates are "filthy." **metū**: what use of the ablative with the verb **līberō**?

145 **intersum, interesse** (*irreg.*), **interfuī**, to lie or exist between. The subjunctive is used here in a **dum modo** clause of proviso. **nōn feram . . . sinam** (146): the anaphora of **nōn** and the repetition of the notion of forbidding in three verbs of approximately the same meaning emphasize Cicero's assertion.

146 **sinō, sinere** (3), **sīvī, situm**, to allow, let, permit (in the sense of not preventing). **Magna**: construe with **grātia** (147), the subject of **habenda est**. The agent, if expressed, would be in the form **ā nōbīs**, since **grātiam habēre** ("to feel grateful") takes the dative.

147 **huic ipsī**: these words refer to Jupiter Stator, the god in whose temple the Senate was meeting. **antīquissimō**: the superlative is appropriate here (compare above, line 121) because, according to tradition, the temple to Jupiter Stator was vowed by Rome's founder and first king, Romulus, when he called upon the god to stay (hence the name Stator) the rout of his Roman troops that were being hard pressed in an assault upon the city by the Sabines.

148 *__**taeter, taetra, taetrum**__, foul, revolting. *__**horribilis, -is, -e**__, terrifying, dreadful. *__**īnfestus, -a, -um**__ (+ *dat.*), hostile, dangerous.

149 **totiēns**, so often, so many times. **effugiō, effugere** (3), **effūgī**, to escape, avoid. **in ūnō homine**: these words assign the blame for the danger to the state to "a single individual" (i.e., Catiline), and they are to be taken closely with the verb **est . . . perīclitanda** (150). Translate freely "a single individual must not repeatedly (lit., too often) be the source of danger to the supreme safety of the state."

150 **perīclitor, perīclitārī** (1), **perīclitātus sum**, to put in peril, endanger. Is the gerundive of a transitive deponent verb active or passive in meaning? **quam diū**, as long as. **cōnsulī dēsignātō**: i.e., in the latter half of the year 64 B.C.

151 **īnsidior, īnsidiārī** (1), **īnsidiātus sum** (+ *dat.*), to make a treacherous attack (on), plot (against). *__**dīligentia, -ae**__ (*f*), carefulness, watchfulness.

152 **proximīs comitiīs cōnsulāribus**: Sallust has earlier (lines 84–86) mentioned this plot of Catiline to assassinate Cicero at the consular elections in 63. **in campō**: see note on line 85.

153 **competītor, competītōris** (*m*), fellow or rival candidate (in an election). Besides the two successful candidates (both plebeians) who were elected consuls for 62, we know the name of a third rival of Catiline, Servius Sulpicius Rufus, who was supported by Cicero but also lost the election. Since Sulpicius, like Catiline, was a patrician, and only one of the two consuls in any given year could be a patrician, it is easy to understand why Cicero threw his support to Sulpicius in the hope of denying office to Catiline. **comprimō, comprimere** (3), **compressī, compressum**, to crush, check. **cōnātus, -ūs** (*m*), effort, attempt. *__**nefārius, -a, -um**__, impious, abominable, wicked.

154 **amīcōrum . . . cōpiīs**: in addition to this private security force composed of Cicero's

28

Catiline is urged to leave Rome and take his band of wicked supporters with him. So long as he remains, Cicero fears for his life. Catiline has tried and failed on numerous occasions for more than a year to murder Cicero, but Cicero escaped with his life thanks to the will of the gods and the vigilance of his friends who served as a bodyguard.

[10.] "Quae cum ita sint, Catilīna, perge quō coepistī, ēgredere aliquandō ex urbe; patent portae; proficīscere. Nimium diū tē imperātōrem tua illa Mānliāna castra dēsīderant. Ēdūc tēcum etiam omnīs tuōs, sī minus, quam plūrimōs; pūrgā urbem. Magnō mē metū līberābis, dum modo inter mē

145 atque tē mūrus intersit. Nōbīscum versārī iam diūtius nōn potes; nōn feram, nōn patiar, nōn sinam. **[11.]** Magna dīs immortālibus habenda est atque huic ipsī Iovī Statōrī, antīquissimō custōdī huius urbis, grātia, quod hanc tam taetram, tam horribilem tamque īnfestam reī pūblicae pestem totiēns iam effūgimus. Nōn est saepius in ūnō homine summa salūs

150 perīclitanda reī pūblicae. Quam diū mihi, cōnsulī dēsignātō, Catilīna, īnsidiātus es, nōn pūblicō mē praesidiō, sed prīvātā dīligentiā dēfendī. Cum proximīs comitiīs cōnsulāribus mē cōnsulem in campō et competītōrēs tuōs interficere voluistī, compressī cōnātūs tuōs nefāriōs amīcōrum praesidiō et cōpiīs, nūllō tumultū pūblicē concitātō; dēnique,

155 quotiēnscumque mē petīstī, per mē tibi obstitī, quamquam vidēbam perniciem meam cum magnā calamitāte reī pūblicae esse coniūnctam.

1. **What act on Catiline's part would free Cicero from great fear?** (141–145)
2. **What did Cicero say his attitude would be if Catiline continued to remain in Rome?** (145–146)
3. **What did Catiline stand to gain by the assassination of Cicero?** (149–151 and 155–156)
4. **At what public event had Catiline most recently made an attempt on Cicero's life?** (152–153)
5. **How had Catiline conducted himself with respect to his rivals for the consulship in 63?** (152–153)
6. **Why does Cicero make so much of his gratitude to the gods and to Jupiter in particular?**

---

friends and retainers, the consul wore a breastplate under his toga on the day of the elections so that the public would be aware of the threat against his life.
*concitō (1), to rouse, stir up, excite.
155 quotiēnscumque, as often as, whenever. petīstī: here "to seek with hostile intent," i.e., "to assault," "attack." obstō, obstāre (1), obstitī, obstātum (+ *dat.*), to stand in the way (of), thwart. *quamquam, although.
156 *coniungō, coniungere (3), coniūnxī, coniūnctum, to join together, link.

157 **Hīsce**: ' = **hīs** (the ablative plural of the demonstrative **hic**) + the enclitic suffix **-ce**
adding emphasis. **ōmen, ōminis** (*n*), omen, portent. Translate, "with these
prophetic words." In a section of the speech not included here and immediately
preceding these concluding remarks, Cicero predicted that the conspiracy would
be exposed and crushed once Catiline set out from Rome. **cum . . . salūte**: this
and the two following **cum** prepositional phrases state the attendant circum-
stances of the imperative **proficīscere** (159). Translate freely, "to the complete
salvation of. . . ."

158 ***exitium, -ī** (*n*), destruction, ruin.

159 **parricīdium, -ī** (*n*), murder (especially of a near relation), assassination. **impius,
-a, -um**, unholy, impious, wicked.

160 ***tēctum, -ī** (*n*), roof, building (a common meaning, by *synecdoche*, the part standing for the whole).

161 **arceō, arcēre** (2), **arcuī**, to keep off, repel. The future here and below (**mactābis,**
164), in place of an expression of petition, denotes the inevitability of the god's
actions.

162 ***latrō, latrōnis** (*m*), robber, bandit, plunderer (of) (+ genitive). **foedus, foederis** (*n*),
league, treaty, compact. **Foedere** and **societāte** are ablatives of means with the
participle **coniūnctōs** (163).

163 **mortuus, -a, -um**, dead. Translate: "in death."

164 **mactō** (1), to honor with sacrifice, (in an extended meaning) afflict, punish.

Remains of the Temple of Jupiter Stator (as seen from the north)

Catiline is invited to bring down ruin upon himself and his followers by having recourse to open warfare. Cicero prays to Jupiter, in whose temple the meeting of the Senate is being held, to destroy the conspirators and preserve the state from harm.

[33.] "Hīsce ōminibus, Catilīna, cum summā reī pūblicae salūte, cum tuā peste ac perniciē cumque eōrum exitiō, quī sē tēcum omnī scelere parricīdiōque iūnxērunt, proficīscere ad impium bellum ac nefārium. Tū,
160 Iuppiter, hunc et huius sociōs ā tuīs cēterīsque templīs, ā tēctīs urbis ac moenibus, ā vītā fortūnīsque cīvium arcēbis; et hominēs bonōrum inimīcōs, hostīs patriae, latrōnēs Italiae, scelerum foedere inter sē ac nefāriā societāte coniūnctōs, aeternīs suppliciīs vīvōs mortuōsque mactābis."

1. **What words does Cicero use to characterize the war Catiline intends to wage?** (159)
2. **How does Cicero characterize Catiline's supporters?** (161–163)
3. **How will divine retribution affect the conspirators?** (163–164)

Remains of the Temple of Jupiter Stator (as seen from the northeast in close-up)

165 **adsīdō, adsīdere** (3), **adsēdī**, to sit down, take a seat. In the Roman Senate, speakers stood up to deliver their remarks. **ut** (*causal*), inasmuch as. The participle **parātus** is to be translated as a simple predicate adjective.

166 **dēmissus, -a, -um**, downcast, humble. **supplex, supplicis**, beseeching, pleading. **quid**: why is the indefinite pronoun **quid** employed here?

167 **ortum**: perfect passive participle modifying **sē**, the accusative subject of the following indirect statement (**sē . . . īnstituisse**), which continues the summary of Catiline's remarks and depends upon a verb of saying or asserting that is easily understood after **postulāre**. The demonstrative adjective **eā** (with **familiā**, an ablative of source) and adverb **ita** prepare the way for the **ut** clause of result (168).

168 **in spē**: "in prospect"; with the verb **habēre**, translate "to count upon," "to expect." In this context, a suitable English idiom for **omnia bona** is "nothing but success." **nē exīstumārent**: the construction reverts to an indirect command after the two intervening indirect statements. The object of this verb is itself an indirect statement, **opus esse** (170), while the person who experiences the need (**opus**, lit., "work") is expressed by the dative **sibi**, and the thing needed by the ablative **perditā rē pūblicā** (170). Translate the latter phrase by taking the leading idea from the participle, "destruction of the state." **sibi**: an instance of the so-called indirect use of the reflexive pronoun, which refers here not to the subject of the verb in its own clause (**exīstumārent**, subject **patrēs** = "senators") but to the subject of the leading verb (**postulāre**, resumed from line 166, subject **Catilīna**). **patricius, -a, -um**, patrician. The patricians were the privileged class in the early Republic, but in course of time, these old aristocratic families were forced to yield their monopoly on public and priestly offices by making concessions to families of plebeian status. By this date, a very small number of families that belonged to the patriciate were still in existence. The descriptive adjective here, as usual, is not attached directly to the pronoun but made to modify the noun **hominī** standing in apposition to **sibi** (compare note on line 121).

169 **maiōrum**: "ancestors"; the full expression is **maiōrum nātū**, "greater with respect to birth." **plēbem Rōmānam**: this expression, less inclusive than the more usual **populum Rōmānum**, appears to be chosen deliberately to provide a contrast with **patriciō** above and perhaps to make the claim that Catiline and his family had been champions of the humbler citizens.

170 **perdō, perdere** (3), **perdidī, perditum**, to destroy, ruin. **eam**: i.e., **rem pūblicam**.

171 **inquilīnus, -ī** (*m*), tenant, lodger. Here this noun stands in apposition to **cīvis** and approaches the force of an adjective ("of foreign birth," "of immigrant status"). The intended slur on Cicero's status as a **novus homō** (see note on line 68) and native of the Italian town of Arpinum, to which Roman citizenship had been extended in the preceding century, can perhaps be captured in English by the expression "virtually a naturalized citizen." **Ad hoc**: i.e., to the insult just reported. This prepositional phrase and the noun **maledicta** form the predicate of the verb **adderet**; the conjunction **cum** has been postponed to bring this predicate into prominence. **maledictum, -ī** (*n*), abusive word, insult. ***addō, addere** (3), **addidī, additum**, to add (in a speech or writing).

172 **obstrepō, obstrepere** (3), **obstrepuī, obstrepitum**, to raise a din, shout in disapproval. This and the following historical infinitive, which as usual have the force of imperfects, may be brought out in English by translating "began to. . . ." ***parricīda, -ae** (*m/f*), murderer (especially of a near relation), cutthroat, traitor. **furibundus, -a, -um**, full of rage, wild with fury.

173 **circumveniō, circumvenīre** (4), **circumvēnī, circumventum**, to surround (with hostile intent), beset, ensnare. Catiline uses military terminology to describe the action taken against him by his enemies. **ab inimīcīs**: this ablative of personal agent is to be construed with both **circumventus** and **agor. praeceps, praecipitis**, headfirst, headlong.

174 **restinguō, restinguere** (3), **restīnxī, restīnctum**, to extinguish (a fire or light), quench, quell. Catiline uses the imagery of putting out a fire to describe the radical measures that he has been forced to adopt against his enemies. **Ruīnā** ("the collapse of a building") alludes to the technique of fighting a fire by pulling down the buildings in the fire's path to prevent it from spreading. The *metaphor* is best brought out in English as follows: "I shall quench the flames that engulf me (**incendium meum**) by general destruction."

RESUMPTION OF SALLUST'S *BELLUM CATILINAE*

Catiline protests his innocence of the charges leveled by Cicero. His attempt to hurl slander at Cicero is met with an angry protest from the senators. Catiline reacts to this outcry by making a veiled threat that he will seek revenge by bringing about general destruction.

165 **[31b.]** Sed ubi ille adsēdit, Catilīna, ut erat parātus ad dissimulanda omnia, dēmissō voltū, vōce supplicī postulāre ā patribus coepit nē quid dē sē temere crēderent; eā familiā ortum, ita sē ab adulēscentiā vītam īnstituisse ut omnia bona in spē habēret; nē exīstumārent sibi patriciō hominī, cuius ipsīus atque maiōrum plūruma beneficia in plēbem
170 Rōmānam essent, perditā rē pūblicā opus esse, cum eam servāret M. Tullius, inquilīnus cīvis urbis Rōmae. Ad hoc maledicta alia cum adderet, obstrepere omnēs, hostem atque parricīdam vocāre. Tum ille furibundus: "Quōniam quidem circumventus," inquit, "ab inimīcīs praeceps agor, incendium meum ruīnā restinguam."

1. With what attitude did Catiline begin his defense? (165–166)
2. Why did Catiline lay such stress on his ancestry? (167–171)

"Cicero and Catiline in the Senate" (19th century painting by Cesari Maccari)

175 **ex cūriā**: = **ex senātū**, not "out of the Senate House" (Curia Hostilia, see plan, p. 6), since we know that the Senate met on this occasion in the Temple of Jupiter Stator (see note on line 109). **domum**: what use of the accusative? **prōripiō, prōripere** (3), **prōripuī, prōreptum**, to snatch forth, (with the reflexive **sē**) rush forth. ***volvō, volvere** (3), **volvī, volūtum**, to turn over, roll over, (with **sēcum**) turn over in his mind.

176 **cōnsulī**: dative of reference (disadvantage) to be construed with **īnsidiae**. ***prōcēdō, prōcēdere** (3), **prōcessī, prōcessum**, to go forward, succeed, go well.

177 **mūnītam**: supply **esse** to complete this perfect passive infinitive (construed with **ab** + ablative) in indirect discourse after **intellegēbat** (176). **optumum factū**: "the best course of action," lit., "best with respect to doing" (**factū**, the supine of **faciō**). Optumum is neuter accusative singular, agreeing with the infinitives **augēre** and **antecapere** (178), which are used substantively here as the objects of **crēdēns**.

178 **scrīberentur**: the verb is in the subjunctive because of the prospective nature of the **priusquam** clause. Related to the subjunctive of purpose, the clause here describes a state of affairs that Catiline sought to anticipate. ***antecapiō, antecapere** (3), **antecēpī, anteceptum**, to seize beforehand, obtain in advance. **bellō ūsuī**: the so-called double dative. **forent**: = **futūra essent**, in a relative clause of characteristic.

179 **intempestus, -a, -um**, untimely, (with **nocte**) in the dead of night. **cum paucīs**: according to one source, as many as 300 armed supporters accompanied Catiline. **Cethēgō . . . cēterīsque**: datives governed by the verb **mandat** (180). Gaius Cornelius Cethegus was a junior member of the Senate and, like Catiline, a patrician. He had been tainted by a scandal or two and had a reputation for being reckless and hotheaded. Publius Cornelius Lentulus Sura, also a patrician, was an important figure in the conspiracy and appears to have directed affairs in the city after Catiline's departure from Rome on the night of 8/9 November. He had been consul in 71 B.C., but in the following year the censors judged him unworthy to retain his seat in the Senate. To regain his senatorial rank, he held the praetorship for a second time in 63.

180 **prōmptus, -a, -um**, ready, active, quick to respond.

181 **possent**: subjunctive because the relative clause occurs within an indirect command (the conjunction **ut** has been omitted) after **mandat**. **mātūrō** (1), to hasten, perform in a timely fashion.

182 **sēsē . . . accessūrum** (183) (*supply* **esse**): the construction shifts from indirect commands after **mandat** (180), to an indirect statement governed by a verb of asserting or promising that can be easily supplied to suit the context. **prope diem**, before long, very soon.

184 ***commoror, commorārī** (1), **commorātus sum**, to delay, linger. **apud C. Flaminium**: **apud** with the name of a person = "at the house of," "with." Nothing further is known about this Gaius Flaminius, who is described by Sallust as living in the vicinity of Arretium, a town in northern Etruria (see map, p. 3).

185 **vīcīnitās, vīcīnitātis** (*f*), neighborhood, neighboring parts, district. **exōrnō** (1), to equip or supply thoroughly. **fascēs, fascium** (*m*), a bundle of wooden rods tied with thongs (usually bound around an ax) symbolizing the right of a magistrate possessing **imperium** to inflict punishment (see illustration, p. 35).

187 **Rōmae**: what case? **hostīs**: "public enemies," predicate accusative after the verb **iūdicat**. By this act, the Senate declared Catiline and Manlius outlaws against whom a state of war existed.

188 ***multitūdō, multitūdinis** (*f*), throng, crowd, mass (of individuals involved in the plot). The dative is governed by the verb **statuit**. **quam**: the antecedent is **diem**, here treated as a feminine noun. **licēret**: the subjunctive is employed because this clause stands in virtual indirect discourse; i.e., it reports the provisions of the Senate's decree. **fraus, fraudis** (*f*), harm, detriment.

189 ***discēdō, discēdere** (3), **discessī, discessum** (*with* **ā** + *abl.*), to cease, leave off, (with **ab armīs**) lay down arms. **praeter**: = **praeterquam**, "except," to be taken with **condemnātīs**. ***capitālis, -is, -e** (of crimes, here **rērum**), involving a capital charge, i.e., punishable by death or loss of civil rights through exile. **condemnō** (1), to condemn, sentence (with the genitive of the charge). The dative plural of the participle may be viewed as balancing **multitūdinī** above (188), or it may be construed with **licēret**.

190 **dīlēctus, -ūs** (*m*), levy (of troops), draft. **persequor, persequī** (3), **persecūtus sum**, to follow (with hostile intent), pursue.

Catiline decides on the night following the meeting of the Senate to join his rebel army in Etruria to the north of Rome. Before he leaves, he calls a meeting of his chief lieutenants and instructs them on the role they are to play in his absence.

175 **[32.]** Deinde sē ex cūriā domum prōripuit. Ibi multa ipse sēcum volvēns, quod neque īnsidiae cōnsulī prōcēdēbant et ab incendiō intellegēbat urbem vigiliīs mūnītam, optumum factū crēdēns exercitum augēre ac, priusquam legiōnēs scrīberentur, multa antecapere quae bellō ūsuī forent, nocte intempestā cum paucīs in Mānliāna castra profectus est. Sed Cethēgō
180 atque Lentulō cēterīsque, quōrum cognōverat prōmptam audāciam, mandat, quibus rēbus possent, opēs factiōnis cōnfīrment, īnsidiās cōnsulī mātūrent, caedem, incendia aliaque bellī facinora parent; sēsē prope diem cum magnō exercitū ad urbem accessūrum.

Catiline illegally assumes the trappings of consular office and makes his way to the rebel camp. When news of this reaches Rome, the Senate declares Catiline and Manlius public enemies and sends out one of the consuls, Antonius, with an army to crush the rebellion. The other consul, Cicero, is to watch over the safety of the city.

[36.] Sed ipse paucōs diēs commorātus apud C. Flāminium in agrō
185 Arrētīnō, dum vīcīnitātem anteā sollicitātam armīs exōrnat, cum fascibus atque aliīs imperī īnsignibus in castra ad Mānlium contendit. Haec ubi Rōmae comperta sunt, senātus Catilīnam et Mānlium hostīs iūdicat, cēterae multitūdinī diem statuit, ante quam licēret sine fraude ab armīs discēdere, praeter rērum capitālium condemnātīs. Praetereā dēcernit utī
190 cōnsulēs dīlēctum habeant, Antōnius cum exercitū Catilīnam persequī mātūret, Cicerō urbī praesidiō sit.

1. **What circumstance hastened Catiline's departure to join Manlius?** (175–178)
2. **What tasks did Catiline assign to his supporters in Rome?** (181–182)
3. **What were Catiline's plans for his return to Rome?** (182–183)
4. **To what power did Catiline illegally lay claim when he assumed the *fascēs*?** (185)
5. **What was the effect of the declaration passed by the Senate against Catiline and Manlius?** (187)
6. **How did the Senate attempt to detach supporters from Catiline?** (188-189)

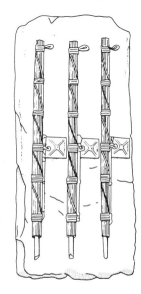

The *fascēs*, a bundle of elm or birch rods bound with a red strap around an ax, the blade of which projected, symbolized the right, originally of the Roman kings and later of Roman magistrates possessing imperium, to inflict corporal or capital punishment by flogging or execution. Each consul was entitled to be accompanied by 12 attendants, called lictors, who each carried the *fascēs*. After laws had been passed in the early Republic granting Roman citizens the right to appeal capital sentences handed down by a magistrate, the ax came to be removed from the *fascēs* when displayed within the boundary of the city. Catiline's adoption of the *fascēs* (lines 185–186) was a bold declaration of usurped imperium.

192 **ut comperī**: "when I ascertained." ***Allobrogēs, Allobrogum** (*m*), a tribe of Gauls living in the Roman province of **Gallia Trānsalpīna** ("lying beyond the Alps"). The territory of this nation was situated east of the Rhône and north of the Isère in what is today the southeast of France. **tumultūs**: this word was used of any warlike disturbance in Italy or Cisalpine Gaul on Italy's northern frontier. The Allobroges had been urged by the conspirators to send cavalry into Italy to join Catiline's army. At the same time, an armed revolt was to take place in Transalpine Gaul (styled here a **bellum Trānsalpīnum**).

193 **ā P. Lentulō**: for his role in the conspiracy, see the note on line 179.

195 **comitemque**: "as a companion"; this noun, agreeing with the subject accusative of the infinitive, is to be translated as a predicate after **adiūnctum esse**. ***adiungō, adiungere** (3), **adiūnxī, adiūnctum**, to add, join, attach. **T. Volturcium**: Titus Volturcius was, according to Sallust, a native of Croton, a town in Brutium in southern Italy (see map, p. 2), and he later testified against the conspirators under a grant of immunity after his arrest (230–236). **ad Catilīnam**: "for Catiline." Sallust and Cicero both preserve the text of a letter that was written by Lentulus and given to Volturcius for delivery to Catiline.

196 **ut, quod . . .** : the **ut** clause is to be construed with **facultātem** ("chance or opportunity to have such and such accomplished"), while **id**, standing in apposition to the statement contained in the **ut** clause, is understood as the antecedent of both **quod** clauses.

197 **tōta rēs**: i.e., the conspiracy as a whole.

198 **manifestō** (*with verbs of discovery or detecting*): "in the act," "undeniably." ***dēprehendō, dēprehendere** (3), **dēprehendī, dēprehēnsum**, to detect, discover, bring to light, catch (in the act).

199 **hesternus, -a, -um**, of yesterday. **hesternō diē**: "yesterday," (in this instance) 2 December. **L. Flaccum . . . C. Pomptīnum**: both men had prior military experience and were well suited to the task assigned to them by Cicero.

200 **reī pūblicae**: what use of the genitive?

201 **quid . . . placēret**: this indirect question supplies the object of **ostendī**.

202 **preaclārus, -a, -um**, illustrious, fine, noble, honorable. **sentīrent**: subjunctive because the **quī** clause is causal. **recūsātiō, recūsātiōnis** (*f*), refusal.

203 **advesperāscit, advesperāscere** (3), **advesperāvit** (*always impersonal*), evening approaches, twilight is coming on. ***occultē**, secretly. **pontem Mulvium**: this bridge, about three miles north of the Forum, carries the **via Flaminia** (see map, p. 3) across the Tiber River. Once across, the party would take the **via Cassia** to Faesulae.

204 **perveniō, pervenīre** (4), **pervēnī, perventum** (*with ad* + *acc.*), to reach, arrive at. **proximus, -a, -um**, nearby, in the immediate vicinity. **bipertītō** (*adv.* + **esse**), to be divided (in two parts or divisions).

205 **intersum, interesse** (*irreg.*), **interfuī**, to lie between. **interesset**: singular agreeing with the nearer of the two subjects.

206 **suspīciō, suspīciōnis** (*f*), suspicion, inkling. **praefectūrā Reātīnā**: the Sabine town of Reate was administered by the Romans as a prefecture; i.e., local jurisdiction was in the hands of a governor (**praefectus**) sent annually from Rome.

207 **assiduē**, continually, constantly.

209 **tertiā . . . exāctā**: this ablative absolute stating the time of the arrest corresponds to approximately 3 A.M. The Romans divided the hours from sunset to sunrise into four equal parts (of varying length depending upon the season of the year) known as **vigiliae** ("watches").

210 ***comitātus, -ūs** (*m*), escort, retinue. The preposition **cum** denoting accompaniment is optional with the noun **comitātus** when it is modified by an adjective. **ingredior, ingredī** (3), **ingressus sum**, to go onto, enter upon.

211 ***ēdūcō, ēdūcere** (3), **ēdūxī, ēductum**, to draw (swords).

212 **sōlīs**: modifying **praetōribus** (dative with the adjective **nōta**, 211). **interventus, -ūs** (*m*), intervention, active interference in a situation.

213 **sēdō** (1), to quiet, stop.

214 **integrīs signīs**: ablative absolute; **signum** here refers to the wax seal with which each unopened letter was secured.

215 **dīlūcēscō, dīlūcēscere** (3), **dīlūxī**, to dawn, become light (here impersonal). ***dēdūcō, dēdūcere** (3), **dēdūxī, dēductum**, to lead away, conduct.

36

Following Catiline's departure from Rome, his associate, the praetor Pub-
lius Lentulus, continued to recruit new members of the conspiracy and
tried to arrange for an uprising in the Roman province of Transalpine
Gaul to coincide with the outbreak of hostilities in Italy. One of the
Celtic tribes whose territory was situated in Transalpine Gaul, the Allo-
broges, had sent ambassadors to Rome to complain of conditions in their
region before the Senate. These ambassadors were approached by the con-
spirators and later revealed to Cicero the attempt that had been made to
recruit them as participants in the conspiracy. Cicero requested them to
pretend to go along with the proposals of the conspirators, and following
Cicero's instructions the ambassadors persuaded the chief members of the
conspiracy to put in writing their proposal for an alliance between them-
selves and the Allobroges. On the night the ambassadors were to leave
Rome with the documents and an escort furnished by Lentulus and the
others, Cicero arranged for this group to be arrested.

CICERO'S *ORATIO IN L. CATILINAM III*

In a speech delivered to the Roman people on 3 December, the day fol-
lowing the arrest, Cicero recounts how he sent the praetors Flaccus and
Pomptinus to seize the conspirators and the ambassadors of the Allobroges
at the Mulvian Bridge on their way north to Catiline's camp in Etruria.

[4.] "Itaque, ut comperī lēgātōs Allobrogum bellī Trānsalpīnī et tumultūs
Gallicī excitandī causā ā P. Lentulō esse sollicitātōs, eōsque in Galliam ad
suōs cīvīs eōdemque itinere cum litterīs mandātīsque ad Catilīnam esse
195 missōs comitemque iīs adiūnctum esse T. Volturcium atque huic ad
Catilīnam esse datās litterās, facultātem mihi oblātam putāvī ut, quod erat
difficillimum quodque ego semper optābam ab dīs immortālibus, tōta rēs
nōn sōlum ā mē, sed etiam ā senātū et ā vōbīs manifestō dēprehenderētur.
[5.] "Itaque hesternō diē L. Flaccum et C. Pomptīnum praetōrēs,
200 fortissimōs atque amantissimōs reī pūblicae virōs, ad mē vocāvī, rem
exposuī, quid fierī placēret ostendī. Illī autem, quī omnia dē rē pūblicā
praeclāra atque ēgregia sentīrent, sine recūsātiōne ac sine ūllā morā
negōtium suscēpērunt et, cum advesperāsceret, occultē ad pontem
Mulvium pervēnērunt atque ibi in proximīs vīllīs ita bipertītō fuērunt, ut
205 Tiberis inter eōs et pōns interesset. Eōdem autem et ipsī sine cuiusquam
suspīciōne multōs fortīs virōs ēdūxerant, et ego ex praefectūrā Reātīnā
complūrīs dēlēctōs adulēscentīs, quōrum operā ūtor assiduē in reī pūblicae
praesidiō, cum gladiīs mīseram.
[6.] "Interim tertiā ferē vigiliā exāctā, cum iam pontem Mulvium magnō
210 comitātū lēgātī Allobrogum ingredī inciperent ūnāque Volturcius, fit in eōs
impetus; ēdūcuntur et ab illīs gladiī et ā nostrīs. Rēs praetōribus erat nōta
sōlīs, ignōrābātur ā cēterīs. Tum interventū Pomptīnī atque Flaccī pugna,
quae erat commissa, sēdātur. Litterae, quaecumque erant in eō comitātū,
integrīs signīs praetōribus trāduntur; ipsī comprehēnsī ad mē, cum iam
215 dīlūcēsceret, dēdūcuntur."

1. **Where were the Allobroges headed on the night of their arrest?** (193–194)
2. **Why was Cicero so anxious to place the traveling party under arrest?** (194–198)
3. **How was the ambush at the bridge arranged by the praetors?** (203–205)
4. **At approximately what time was the arrest made?** (209)
5. **What did the traveling party do when the soldiers closed in on the bridge?** (211)

216 ***propere**, hastily, quickly.

217 **illum**: i.e., Cicero.

218 **intellegens**: this participle and **dubitans** below (219) are causal; **intellegens** has as its object an indirect statement, while the object of **dubitans** is an indirect question. ***patefaciō, patefacere** (3), **patefēcī, patefactum**, to lay open, disclose, expose. ***ēripiō, ēripere** (3), **ēripuī, ēreptum** (+ *abl. of separation*), to snatch away, deliver, rescue.

219 **porrō**, at the same time, on the other hand. **anxius, -a, -um**, worried, troubled. **tantīs cīvibus dēprehēnsīs**: best taken as an ablative absolute balancing **coniūrā-tiōne patefactā** above (218); **tantīs** ("such great") is used especially in reference to the praetor Lentulus and the senator Cethegus, both of whom were patricians.

220 **quid . . . esset**: "what ought to be done." **Opus** (signifying "need") is construed here, as often, with the ablative of the perfect passive participle. **Quid**, however, the logical object of the participle, is made the grammatical subject because it is interrogative, and **opus** becomes a predicate nominative. **poenam**: understood is **fore** (= **futūram esse**) from below (221) to complete this first indirect statement. The predicate consists of the double dative **sibi onerī**, and an adversative conjunction is to be supplied before **inpūnitātem**. **inpūnitās, inpūnitātis** (*f*), freedom from punishment, remission of punishment, granting of pardon.

221 **perdundae reī pūblicae**: genitive of tendency, "would serve to destroy the state."

222 **Lentulum . . . Gabīnium**: on Lentulus and Cethegus, see note on line 179. Lucius Statilius and Publius Gabinius Capito were members of the equestrian order rather than senators. Both were to oversee the fires that were to be set in Rome, and Gabinius had played an active role in the negotiations with the Allobroges. **itemque**: **item** is used to set apart the last individual mentioned in the series as somehow distinct from the rest. In this instance, as Sallust goes on to state (224–225), Marcus Caeparius, a minor figure in the conspiracy, who is identified as a native of Terracina, a town in Latium (**Terracīnēnsem**), managed to escape from Rome before he could be brought before the Senate, while the other four answered the summons to appear. Caeparius was later captured and placed under house arrest after the Senate adjourned (247–248).

223 **in Apūliam**: on the location of Apulia, see note on line 89. ***servitium, -ī** (*n*), the condition of being a slave, slavery, (here used in a concrete sense) slaves.

225 ***indicium, -ī** (*n*), disclosure, evidence. **profugiō, profugere** (3), **profūgī**, to run away, make one's escape.

226 **perdūcō, perdūcere** (3), **perdūxī, perductum**, to conduct, lead (before a court or other authority). **relicuōs**: an older spelling for **reliquōs**. **in aedem Concordiae**: this was the place chosen for the meeting of the Senate. The Temple of Concord, built in 367 B.C. and refurbished in 121 B.C., was located at the foot of the Capitoline Hill and overlooked the Roman Forum (see plan, p. 6).

227 ***Eō** (*adv.*): i.e., to the Temple of Concord. Likewise **eōdem** below (229). **advocō** (1), to summon, call together, convoke. **frequentia, -ae** (*f*), concourse, throng. The ablative is best taken as an ablative absolute.

228 **intrōdūcō, intrōdūcere** (3), **intrōdūxī, intrōductum**, to lead or bring in, usher (into someone's presence). Contrary to Sallust's assertion here, Cicero states that Volturcius was first brought before the Senate **sine Gallīs**. **scrīnium, -ī** (*n*), a box or case for holding letters or papers.

229 **adferō, adferre** (*irreg.*), **attulī, allātum**, to bring with one, convey.

After some hesitation, Cicero decides to call the leading members of the conspiracy before the Senate and present the written evidence of their guilt, which consisted of the documents confiscated when the Allobroges and their escort were taken into custody the night before.

[46.] Quibus rēbus cōnfectīs omnia properē per nūntiōs cōnsulī dēclārantur. At illum ingēns cūra atque laetitia simul occupāvēre. Nam laetābātur intellegēns coniūrātiōne patefactā cīvitātem perīculīs ēreptam esse; porrō autem anxius erat, dubitāns in maxumō scelere tantīs cīvibus
220 dēprehēnsīs quid factō opus esset; poenam illōrum sibi onerī, inpūnitātem perdundae reī pūblicae fore crēdēbat. Igitur cōnfirmātō animō vocārī ad sēsē iubet Lentulum, Cethēgum, Statilium, Gabīnium, itemque Caepārium Terracīnēnsem, quī in Apūliam ad concitanda servitia proficīscī parābat. Cēterī sine morā veniunt; Caepārius, paulō ante domō ēgressus, cognitō
225 indiciō ex urbe profūgerat. Cōnsul Lentulum, quod praetor erat, ipse manū tenēns in senātum perdūcit; relicuōs cum custōdibus in aedem Concordiae venīre iubet. Eō senātum advocat, magnāque frequentiā eius ōrdinis Volturcium cum lēgātīs intrōdūcit; Flaccum praetōrem scrīnium cum litterīs quās ā lēgātīs accēperat eōdem adferre iubet.

1. What emotions did Cicero experience when the conspirators had fallen into his trap? What choices did he face? (217–221)
2. Why did Caeparius fail to answer the summons to appear before the Senate? (224–225)
3. Why did Cicero personally escort Lentulus to the Senate? (225)
4. What was the praetor Flaccus instructed to convey to the meeting of the Senate? (228–229)
5. For what reason did Cicero want to bring the matter before the Senate, even though he had been granted extraordinary powers previously by the Senate to take whatever steps he deemed necessary to preserve the safety of the state?

Opposite: *The Mulvian Bridge (west side).* Above: *Podium of the Temple of Concord (western end of the Forum). The road in the foreground dates from 1882. Beyond, modern buildings on the eastern face of the Capitol.*

230 **dē ... dē ... quid**: notice the variety of structures completing **interrogātus**.
quid ... cōnsilī (231): "what sort of plan"; a partitive genitive frequently follows words such as **quid**, **satis**, and **quantum**. **quā dē causā**: Latin prepositions of one syllable introducing phrases containing a modified noun frequently are postponed, i.e., are placed between the adjective (here the interrogative **quā**) and noun that make up the phrase.

231 **habuisset**: identify this use of the subjunctive. **prīmō ... post** (232): in rhetorical prose, such "signposts" signal the stages of an argument. **fingere ... dissimulāre**: Volturcius (230) is the nominative subject of these historical infinitives.

232 **fidē pūblicā**: "on the government's guarantee (of immunity)"; ablative of attendant circumstance. ***utī**: = **ut** (+ indicative). **aperit, docet**: historical presents, "reveals ... states."

233 **sē ... scīre** (234): indirect statement with **docet**. **adscīscō, adscīscere** (3), **adscīvī, adscītum**, to admit (as an associate or the like). **socium adscītum**: "admitted as a confederate."

234 **lēgātōs**: i.e., of the Allobroges. **tantummodo**: the adverb **tantum** is strengthened by **modo**, "merely." **audīre**: a complementary infinitive governed by **solitum (esse)**, which continues the indirect statement introduced by **docet**: "that he had been accustomed to hear that. . . . "

237 **Eadem**: accusative object of **fatentur**, "make the same confession." **coarguō, coarguere** (3), **coarguī**, to refute, prove guilty.

238 **sermōnibus**: the relative clause **quōs ... solitus erat** seems to suggest that these conversations of Lentulus were habitual. The following infinitive clauses are indirect statements completing the quoting idea suggested in **sermōnibus**. **librīs Sibyllīnīs**: the Sibylline Oracles, contained in three volumes, which (legend said) the Sibyl of Cumae sold to Rome's last king, Tarquinius Superbus, could be consulted only by an act of the Senate. Lentulus, therefore, could be aware of this prophecy only at second hand.

239 **tribus Cornēliīs**: dative of reference. The first two Corneliī had been L. Cornelius Cinna (despotic consul 87–84 B.C.) and L. Cornelius Sulla (consul 88 and 80, dictator 82–79). **portendō, portendere** (3), **portendī, portentum**, to foretell, predict.

240 **foret** (archaic): = **esset**; subjunctive in a subordinate clause in indirect discourse. **potior, potīrī** (4), **potītus sum** (+ *abl. or, as here, gen.*), to get possession of. **ab incēnsō Capitōliō**, "from the burning of the Capitol" (6 July 83 B.C.), a common dating formula using the participle instead of an abstract noun.

241 **illum ... annum**: i.e., the present year; **hic** is replaced by **ille** in indirect discourse. **vīcēsimus, -a, -um**, twentieth. **quem ... cruentum fore** (242): indirect statement completing **respondissent** (242). **prōdigium, -ī** (*n*), prophetic sign, omen, portent (usually in a threatening sense). **haruspex, haruspicis** (*m*), soothsayer (trained in the Etruscan art of interpreting signs sent by the gods by inspecting the entrails of sacrificed animals and by observing bolts of lightning).

242 **fore**: = **futūrum esse**.

243 **perlegō, perlegere** (3), **perlēgī, perlēctum**, to read through. **prius**: i.e., before the messages were opened in front of the gathered senators. **signum, -ī** (*n*), sign, (here) seal (sender's identification mark pressed into a wax seal with which one secures tied messages). **cognōvissent**: "had acknowledged." The subjunctive with **cum** temporal must follow secondary sequence (hence **cognōvissent**, pluperfect) when the main verb (**dēcernit**, 244) is in the historical present.

244 **abdicō** (1), to renounce. **abdicātō magistrātū**: ablative absolute with temporal force, "after . . ." Lentulus' resignation would be voluntary, the result of pressure from his colleagues in the Senate; Roman law did not recognize impeachment.

245 ***custōdia, -ae** (*f*), detention, arrest. **in līberīs custōdiīs** (244–245): "in free custody," i.e., house arrest. The Romans had no jails for this purpose. **habeantur**: explain this use of the subjunctive. **P. Lentulō Spinthērī**: dative, indirect object completing **trāduntur** (248). **aedīlis, aedīlis** (*m*), aedile (annually elected magistrate next in rank below the praetors). Aediles were ministers of public works.

246 **C. Caesarī ... M. Crassō**: Julius Caesar (consul 59 B.C.) was praetor-elect in 63, and three years later he and Marcus Crassus (consul 70 and 55) joined with Pompey to form the so-called first triumvirate, a political coalition that dominated Roman politics throughout most of the following decade. Some supposed in 63 that both Crassus and Caesar were secretly involved in Catiline's conspiracy. Thus it has been suggested that the decision to place two of the conspirators in their custody

40

At the tense meeting convened in the Temple of Concord on 3 December, the Senate hears the evidence of Volturcius after promising him immunity. He implicates a number of prominent Romans in the plot.

230 **[47.]** Volturcius interrogātus dē itinere, dē litterīs, postrēmō quid aut quā dē causā cōnsilī habuisset, prīmō fingere alia, dissimulāre dē coniūrātiōne; post, ubi fidē pūblicā dīcere iussus est, omnia utī gesta erant aperit, docetque sē, paucīs ante diēbus ā Gabīniō et Caepāriō socium adscītum, nihil amplius scīre quam lēgātōs, tantummodo audīre solitum ex Gabīniō
235 P. Autrōnium, Ser. Sullam, L. Varguntēium, multōs praetereā in eā coniūrātiōne esse.

The Allobrogian envoys corroborate Volturcius' evidence regarding the others and report frequent boasts Lentulus made to them about his own political expectations. He has pinned his hopes on Rome's holiest collection of prophecies, the writings of the Sibyl of Cumae.

Eadem Gallī fatentur ac Lentulum dissimulantem coarguunt praeter litterās sermōnibus quōs ille habēre solitus erat; ex librīs Sibyllīnīs rēgnum Rōmae tribus Cornēliīs portendī; Cinnam atque Sullam anteā, sē
240 tertium esse cui fātum foret urbis potīrī; praetereā ab incēnsō Capitōliō illum esse vīcēsimum annum, quem saepe ex prōdigiīs haruspicēs respondissent bellō cīvīlī cruentum fore.

Condemned by their own letters, the conspirators are given over to house arrest, and the praetor Lentulus resigns his office in disgrace.

Igitur perlēctīs litterīs, cum prius omnēs signa sua cognōvissent, senātus dēcernit utī abdicātō magistrātū Lentulus itemque cēterī in līberīs
245 custōdiīs habeantur. Itaque Lentulus P. Lentulō Spinthērī, quī tum aedīlis erat, Cethēgus Q. Cornificiō, Statilius C. Caesārī, Gabīnius M. Crassō, Caepārius—nam is paulō ante ex fugā retrāctus erat—Cn. Terentiō senātōrī trāduntur.

1. **What four questions was Volturcius asked during his interrogation?** (230–231)
2. **What was his first response to these questions?** (231)
3. **What led him to change his form of response?** (232)
4. **What did Volturcius keep hearing from Gabinius?** (234–236)
5. **Does Sallust imply, in using the verb *fatentur* (237), that the *Gallī* were under any pressure in making their report? Is there any clear indication that their evidence was not willingly given? Select evidence for your answer carefully.**
6. **What special sense does the context suggest to you for the word *ex* (238)?**
7. **What significance did the burning of the Capitol have in Lentulus' argument?** (240–242)
8. **What evidence seems to have had the most significance for the Senate?** (243)
9. **What two decisions did the Senate make?** (244–245) **How was the second of these carried out?** (245–248)

---

may have been intended to force them to declare their loyalty to one side or the other unequivocally.
247 **retrahō, retrahere** (3), **retrāxī, retrāctum**, to drag back, bring back.

249 **lēgātīs ... et T. Volturciō**: dative, indirect objects with **dēcernuntur** (250).

250 **conprobō** (1), to approve, sanction. ***lībertus, -ī** (m), freedman. ***paucī ex** (+ *abl.*): "a few of"; this partitive formula is also used with other words expressing quantity or number such as **ūnus, multī,** and **nēmō. paucī ... partim** (252): = **aliī ... aliī**; thus **partim** distinguishes the subject of **exquīrēbant** (252) as separate from the subject of **sollicitābant** (252).

251 **opifex, opificis** (m), manual laborer. **vīcus, -ī** (m), neighborhood, street, district. **ad eum ēripiundum**: gerundive of purpose, "to free him."

252 **exquīrō, exquīrere** (3), **exquīsīvī, exquīsītum,** to search for. **ducēs multitūdinum**: the plural of **multitūdō** ("mobs," "gangs") is rare. Leaders of armed gangs played an increasing role in the politics of the city at this time. While the Senate tried, by a decree of 64 B.C., to reduce their power, nonetheless demagogues vied for power in bloody street battles with growing frequency, often intimidating the public authorities.

253 **rem pūblicam vexāre**: "to cause public disturbances."

254 **familiam**: "his household (slaves)." **ōrābat in audāciam**: = **ut audācēs essent**.

255 **sēsē**: reduplicated form of **sē** with no change of meaning or added emphasis; reflexive, referring to the subject of **ōrābat** (254). **inrumpō, inrumpere** (3), **inrūpī, inruptum,** to break in, force an entry.

256 ***dispōnō, dispōnere** (3), **disposuī, dispositum,** to station, post. **ut ... monēbat** (257): identify this use of **ut** with the indicative. Notice that a compound subject such as **rēs atque tempus** may take a singular verb.

257 ***referō, referre** (*irreg.*), **rettulī, relātum,** to bring back, report, propose (a subject) for debate. **refert quid**: "referred to them the question what. ... ," historical present. **quid ... placeat**: identify the structure.

258 **Sed**: "But of course." **eōs ... contrā rem pūblicam fēcisse** (259): "that they had acted as enemies of the state" and therefore, in accordance with the Senate's earlier undertaking, had relinquished any claim to the protection of Roman law; see above, lines 187–189.

259 **sententiam rogātus**: **rogāre** is completed, when active, with two accusatives, one of the person and one of the thing asked, e.g., **cōnsul Sīlānum sententiam rogāvit**; when passive, **rogāre** keeps the accusative object of the thing, as here.

260 **cōnsul dēsignātus**: "consul-elect," as a result of the previous summer's regular elections.

261 **sī dēprehēnsī forent**: "if they should be caught." On **forent**, see note on line 240 above. The pluperfect subjunctive represents the future perfect indicative of direct discourse.

262 **supplicium, -ī** (n), punishment, torture. **supplicium sūmere,** to impose the death penalty (+ **dē** + ablative of the person punished).

The Temple of Concord, overlooking the place where the Senate met on 3–5 December (depicted on a sestertius of Tiberius)

42

The populace is outraged at the idea of a civil war in which it may suffer and showers the consul Cicero with thanks and congratulations for apprehending the conspirators. On 4 December, the Senate hears evidence from a conspirator who had been arrested trying to flee north to Catiline. The arrested conspirator, turned informer, tries to implicate Marcus Crassus in the plot, but the Senate is reluctant to credit the accusations made against such a powerful figure. Even Caesar, praetor-elect for 62, finds himself the subject of bitter accusations and rumored lies. Meanwhile, ranging about the byways of Rome, desperate associates attempt to free the principal conspirators.

[50.] Dum haec in senātū aguntur et dum lēgātīs Allobrogum et T.
250 Volturciō, conprobātō eōrum indiciō, praemia dēcernuntur, lībertī et paucī
ex clientibus Lentulī dīvorsīs itineribus opificēs atque servitia in vīcīs ad
eum ēripiundum sollicitābant; partim exquīrēbant ducēs multitūdinum,
quī pretiō rem pūblicam vexāre solitī erant. Cethēgus autem per nūntiōs
familiam atque lībertōs suōs, lēctōs et exercitātōs, ōrābat in audāciam, ut
255 grege factō cum tēlīs ad sēsē inrumperent.

The consul Cicero recognized that these preparations would blow up into yet another storm threatening the already-weakened ship of state. What if Catiline's army were to make its move at a time when the government was distracted by its struggle to survive? Cicero saw that decisive action must be taken without delay, and the very next day, on 5 December, he convened the Senate to decide the fate of the five arrested conspirators.

Cōnsul ubi ea parārī cognōvit, dispositīs praesidiīs ut rēs atque tempus
monēbat, convocātō senātū refert quid dē eīs fierī placeat quī in custōdiam
trāditī erant. Sed eōs paulō ante frequēns senātus iūdicāverat contrā rem
pūblicam fēcisse. Tum D. Iūnius Sīlānus, prīmus sententiam rogātus quod
260 eō tempore cōnsul dēsignātus erat, dē eīs quī in custōdiīs tenēbantur et
praetereā dē L. Cassiō, P. Fūriō, P. Umbrēnō, Q. Anniō, sī dēprehēnsī
forent, supplicium sūmundum dēcrēverat.

1. How did Lentulus' supporters react to his being imprisoned? (250–253)
2. Why would they have chosen *opificēs* (251) to help them?
3. How did Cethegus' reaction to his imprisonment (253–255) differ from that of Lentulus? How did it resemble it?
4. What evidence are we given to believe that Cethegus was preparing for trouble? (254)
5. In what two ways did Cicero respond to the threat to public peace? (256–258)
6. What does Sallust mean by the clause *ut rēs atque tempus monēbat* (256–257)? What is the effect of phrasing this idea as a personification?
7. Why was Silanus the first senator to be asked for his opinion? (259–260)
8. What was Silanus' opinion? (260–262)
9. The lines are now drawn: some conspirators (two of them senators) are in custody and can be held for trial at a later date. They can also be executed as enemies of the state or let go on the grounds that they have not really done anything yet as hostile to Rome as has Catiline. Decide how you think the Senate should vote, and give appropriate evidence to support your decision.

263 **omnīs hominēs . . . vacuōs esse decet** (264): the impersonal verb **decet** takes an indirect statement. ***patrēs cōnscrīptī**: this titular epithet signifies the senators' right to sit as duly "enrolled" by the quinquennial revisions of the Senate lists by the Board of Censors. **dubius, -a, -um**, ambiguous, moot. ***cōnsultō** (1) (+ **dē** + *abl.*), to inquire into, ponder.

264 **odium, -ī** (*n*), hatred. Notice that the four nouns **odiō, amīcitiā, īrā**, and **misericordiā** name emotional responses, which Caesar here condemns. **vacuus, -a, -um**, free (from) (+ **ab** + ablative). **Haud facile**: the strong contrast is heightened by the prominent positioning of the words.

265 **vērum, -ī** (*n*), the truth. ***prōvideō, prōvidēre** (2), **prōvīdī, prōvīsum**, to look ahead to, discern. Both **prōvidet** and **officiunt** are in the general present, so that **ubi** = "whenever," "at times when." **illa**: i.e., the emotions just named. **officiō, officere** (3), **offēcī, offectūm**, to stand in the way. **neque quisquam**: = et nēmō. **omnium**: partitive genitive with **quisquam**.

266 **lubīdinī . . . ūsuī**: dative objects of **pāruit**. **simul et**: "both . . . and. . . ." **Lubīdō** refers to the emotions just named, while **ūsus** responds to **animus**; translate freely, "impulse/passion . . . sense of what is needed." **pāruit**: "has obeyed," "has served." Because the sentence is cast in the present, this perfect has the sense of our present perfect; it is called gnomic because it expresses a general truth (Greek *gnōmē*). **Ubi intenderis**: the perfect subjunctive of the indefinite 2nd person singular makes the **ubi** clause general, "Whenever a person has applied close attention." **valet**: the subject is **animus** understood. Notice the balancing **animus nihil valet** in the next line.

267 **possidet**: supply some object such as **tē**. **ea . . . valet**: the asyndeton varies this apodosis (main clause) and, with the parallelism, heightens the contrast between the subjects **ea** (= **lubīdō**) and **animus**. **dominor, dominārī** (1), **dominātus sum**, to rule. **nihil valet**: an intransitive verb may take as an object the accusative of a neuter pronoun or adjective of indefinite meaning; **nihil valet** is an example of this cognate accusative, like our "avails nothing"; here, "has no strength."

268 **D. Sīlānum . . . dīxisse** (269): an indirect statement governed by **certō sciō**; the object of **dīxisse** is (**ea**) **quae dīxerit**. **strēnuus, -a, -um**, active, vigorous. ***certō**, certainly, surely. **dīxerit**: perfect subjunctive in a subordinate clause in indirect discourse. **studium, -ī** (*n*), zeal. **studiō**: causal ablative governing the objective genitive **reī pūblicae** (269).

269 **illum**: i.e., Silanus; accusative subject of **exercēre** (270).

270 **eōs mōrēs . . . cognōvī**: **eōs** and **eam** ("such") are predicate adjectives linked to the two accusatives governed by **cognōvī** by an understood **esse**. **modestia, -ae** (*f*), moderation.

271 **mihi**: indirect object of **vidētur** (272). **fierī**: perhaps weak enough here to mean little more than **esse**.

272 **aliēnus, -a, -um**, foreign to (+ **ab** + ablative.).

273 **subigō, subigere** (3), **subēgī, subāctum**, to compel. **cōnsulem dēsignātum**: accusative in apposition to **tē** (272). **novom**: = **novum**; see note on **volgus** (38).

274 **supervacuāneum est**: "it is superfluous." **disserō, disserere** (3), **disseruī, dissertum** (+ **dē** + *abl.*), to discuss, comment on. **cum . . . sint** (275): causal, "since . . . " **dīligentia, -ae** (*f*), carefulness. The ablative here is causal.

275 **tanta**: "as great as we see protecting us here."

276 **id**: this pronoun anticipates and stands in apposition to the following indirect statement, **mortem aerumnārum requiem . . . esse** (277). **rēs habet**: "the present issue involves." ***lūctus, -ūs** (*m*), grief. **miseriae, -ārum** (*f pl*), times of affliction. Pluralized abstract nouns become concrete.

277 **aerumnae, -ārum** (*f*), tribulation, suffering. Here, the genitive is objective with **requiem**. **requiēs, requiētis** (*acc.* **requiem**) (*f*), rest, relief. **cruciātus, -ūs** (*m*), torture, punishment. **eam**: = **mortem**, accusative subject of **dissolvere** (278), continuing the indirect statement after **dīcere** (276).

278 **dissolvō, dissolvere** (3), **dissolvī, dissolūtum**, to let go, release. **ultrā**: "after death" (lit., "beyond that"). **cūrae . . . gaudiō**: datives of purpose with **locum**. **gaudium, -ī** (*n*), joy.

As president of the meeting, Cicero was obliged by custom to call first for the opinion of D. Junius Silanus, consul-elect for 62. Silanus urged that the five conspirators, and any others if caught, should be put to death. Sallust does not quote Silanus' speech in full. He does, however, present at considerable length speeches of the sort (huiuscemodī verba) that we are to believe two speakers, Julius Caesar and Cato, did in fact deliver. Just before quoting Caesar's speech, Sallust warns us that it shook Silanus' confidence in his own opening attitude. Caesar argues that reason must prevail over emotion at a time when all emotions are under severe strain.

[51.] "Omnīs hominēs, patrēs cōnscrīptī, quī dē rēbus dubiīs cōnsultant, ab odiō, amīcitiā, īrā atque misericordiā vacuōs esse decet. Haud facile
265 animus vērum prōvidet ubi illa officiunt, neque quisquam omnium lubīdinī simul et ūsuī pāruit. Ubi intenderis ingenium, valet; sī lubīdō possidet, ea dominātur, animus nihil valet.

Caesar goes on to cite examples from Roman history, illustrating the successful use of reason in reaching decisions favorable to Rome's interests. His examples, Caesar explains, teach the senators on this occasion how the guilt of the conspirators in custody must not matter more with them than do their own dignity (dignitās) and good reputation (fāma). He counsels a punishment strictly within the limits of the law. Some of the speakers preceding him had tried to inflame the debate with forecasts of horror and doom. Caesar does not argue that the traitors have not committed the worst of all crimes. The senators must realize, however, that an unusual punishment now will seem to others later to be arrogant cruelty. Caesar speculates on Silanus' reasons for proposing the death penalty.

"D. Sīlānum, virum fortem atque strēnuum, certō sciō quae dīxerit studiō reī pūblicae dīxisse, neque illum in tantā rē grātiam aut inimīcitiās
270 exercēre: eōs mōrēs, eamque modestiam virī cognōvī. Vērum sententia eius mihi nōn crūdēlis—quid enim in tālīs hominēs crūdēle fierī potest?—sed aliēna ā rē pūblicā nostrā vidētur. Nam profectō aut metus aut iniūria tē subēgit, Sīlāne, cōnsulem dēsignātum, genus poenae novom dēcernere.

Fear is unnecessary, claims Caesar, and the arrested conspirators may decide that death is not really a punishment to them now.

"Dē timōre supervacuāneum est disserere, cum praesertim dīligentiā
275 clārissumī virī cōnsulis tanta praesidia sint in armīs. Dē poenā possum equidem dīcere, id quod rēs habet, in lūctū atque miseriīs mortem aerumnārum requiem, nōn cruciātum esse; eam cūncta mortālium mala dissolvere; ultrā neque cūrae neque gaudiō locum esse.

1. **Four emotions (odium, amīcitia, īra, and misericordia) are arranged in antithesis in line 264. Why is this figure effective here?**
2. **What importance does Caesar give animus in his view of the problem?** (264–267)
3. **What danger does Caesar see in letting lubīdō dominate a debate?** (266–267)
4. **What is Caesar's real opinion of Silanus' proposal?** (270–272)
5. **What credit does Caesar give to the consul Cicero?** (274–275)
6. **Why does Caesar say that the Senate need not consider fear an issue?** (274–275)
7. **It may be that Caesar overstates his praise of Cicero. If he is using hyperbole, do you think he is speaking ironically? Or has his hyperbole some other purpose?**
8. **How does Caesar characterize death?** (276–278) **How are we to suppose the arrested conspirators see it? What is Caesar's motive for this characterization?**

279 **utī** (= **ut**) . . . **animadvorterētur** (280): indirect command, "that they be punished," impersonal passive.

280 **verber, verberis** (*n*), whip, lash. **animadvorterētur**: = **animadverterētur**, archaic spelling. **An quia . . . ? . . . An quia . . .** ? (282) "Was it because . . . ? Or because . . . ?" Sallust provides even a third suggestion in the varied **Sīn quia. . . .** (283). **lēx Porcia**: the Porcian Law apparently restricted a magistrate's right to flog a citizen without trial.

281 **item**, in like manner, similarly. **condemnātīs cīvibus**: dative of separation with **ēripī** and indirect object of **permittī** (282). **animam ēripī . . . exilium permittī**: accusative and infinitive completions of **iubent** (282).

282 **gravius**: predicate adjective agreeing with the infinitives **verberārī** and **necārī**, here neuter substantives supplying the subject of **est**. **verberō** (1), to whip, thrash, flog. **Quid**: "What (punishment) . . . ?" **autem**: sometimes this conjunction means "but."

283 **nimis**, too, excessively. **facinoris**: genitive completing **convictōs**, "convicted (of)." ****convincō, convincere** (3), **convīcī, convictum**, to convict, find guilty.

284 **quī convenit**: "how is it consistent?" **Quī** is an old ablative that had acquired the force of an adverb, while **convenit** is impersonal. **cum . . . neglēgeris** (285): archaic spelling for the perfect subjunctive **neglēxeris**.

286 **At enim**: "But, you say, . . . " This formula introduces a *rhetorical question* (**quis reprehendet . . .** ?) whose obvious answer ("No one") occurs in the audience's minds only. **in parricīdās**: "against murderers"; with **reī pūblicae**, "destroyers of the state." **dēcrētum erit**: future perfect indicating action in future time but prior with reference to the main verb (**reprehendet**).

287 **Tempus, diēs**: these are not simply synonyms here. While **tempus** most often means time in general, **diēs** in contrast may mean "the lapse of time" or "the passage of days/years." **Tempus . . . moderātur**: Caesar suggests the answer to his own question. **fortūna**: defined by the relative clause following. **lubīdō**: here, "inclination," "fancy," "whim." **gentibus**: the dative, as here, or the accusative is used with **moderārī**. **moderor, moderārī** (1), **moderātus sum**, to govern, be the controlling factor in. **Illīs**: "Those prisoners." **Ille** customarily changes the direction of the reader's attention.

288 **ēvēnerit**: future perfect indicative. **cēterum**: an adverb pointing up the contrast between **illīs** and **vōs**. **quid . . . statuātis** (289): indirect question with **cōnsīderāte**. **in aliōs**: others accused in future of being **parricīdae**. Their punishment will be influenced by the Senate's decision, which will serve as a precedent (**exemplum**).

289 **rēbus bonīs**: here, "good measures." Contrast the usual meaning, "prosperity." **orta sunt**: the tense (gnomic perfect, see note on 266) is general and descriptive, "have arisen" (i.e., this is what has happened as a rule in the past).

290 **ignārus, -a, -um** (+ *gen.*), ignorant, not knowing. **ignārōs eius**: "those who do not understand it (i.e., **imperium**)." **minus bonōs**: "less loyal persons." **pervēnit**: the perfect indicative makes the **ubi** clause general: "whenever. . . . "

291 **exemplum**: Caesar means the harsh punishment under debate. **dignīs**: "deserving of it"; so also **idōneīs**. Thus **indignōs** = "those who do not deserve."

292 **Placet . . .** ?: supply **mihi** (impersonal usage), "Do I recommend . . . ?" **eōs . . . exercitum**: the chiasmus serves to point up the *antithesis* between simply letting the prisoners go and the impact such an act would have on Catiline's army.

293 ****cēnseō, cēnsēre** (2), **cēnsuī, cēnsum**, to be of the opinion. **ita cēnseō**: "my opinion is this, that. . . . " **pūblicandās . . . habendōs**: supply **esse** with both gerundives; the two resulting periphrastic infinitives are the verbs in indirect statements completing **cēnseō**. ****pūblicō** (1), to make public property of, confiscate. **pecūniās**: "financial holdings." This is the concrete plural, like **miseriīs** (276). **ipsōs**: "the men themselves."

294 **neu . . . nēve** (295): the construction after **cēnseō** shifts now after the two preceding indirect statements to two negative indirect commands. **quis**: this is the usual shortened form of **aliquis** following **sī, nisi, nē**, and **num**.

295 **cum populō agat**: "debate the matter before the assembly of the people," a stock expression. **quī aliter fēcerit**: Caesar would penalize anyone violating either of his last two proposals. **Fēcerit** is perfect subjunctive indicating a completed act in primary sequence in a subordinate clause in indirect discourse. In the implied direct, **fēcerit** would have appeared in the future perfect indicative. **senātum**: accusative subject of **exīstumāre**, having as its object the following indirect statement. **eum . . . factūrum** (296): supply **esse**, "that he is intending to act."

Roman citizens convicted of capital crimes were ordinarily permitted to go into voluntary exile rather than face execution. Various laws restricted the right of magistrates to flog Roman citizens. Therefore, Silanus seems to have been guided by the law in not recommending flogging but has violated usage in recommending the graver penalty of execution. Caesar questions Silanus' reasoning on this apparent contradiction.

"Sed, per deōs immortālīs, quam ob rem in sententiam nōn addidistī utī
280 prius verberibus in eōs animadvorterētur? An quia lēx Porcia vetat? At aliae lēgēs item condemnātīs cīvibus nōn animam ēripī, sed exilium permittī iubent. An quia gravius est verberārī quam necārī? Quid autem acerbum aut nimis grave est in hominēs tantī facinoris convictōs? Sīn quia levius est, quī convenit in minōre negōtiō lēgem timēre, cum eam in
285 maiōre neglēgeris?

Caesar warns the Senate that it is about to establish a far-reaching precedent. The Senate will not be able to prevent this precedent from being used at some future time against innocent men tried by a court that is not so high-minded and justified as the present Senate.

"At enim quis reprehendet quod in parricīdās reī pūblicae dēcrētum erit? Tempus, diēs, fortūna, cuius lubīdō gentibus moderātur. Illīs meritō accidet quicquid ēvēnerit; cēterum vōs, patrēs cōnscrīptī, quid in aliōs statuātis cōnsīderāte. Omnia mala exempla ex rēbus bonīs orta sunt. Sed
290 ubi imperium ad ignārōs eius aut minus bonōs pervēnit, novom illud exemplum ab dignīs et idōneīs ad indignōs et nōn idōneōs trānsfertur.

Caesar cited several historical examples, both Greek and Roman, to show the danger of establishing by precedent the right to execute citizens who are considered enemies of the state. In his examples, while the populace at first applauded the unlawful executions of hated figures by tyrannical authority, eventually the people turned against these measures with repugnance. Our ancestors, he continues, whose pride and courage Romans do not question, instituted the practice of allowing the condemned the alternative of exile. This current precedent, Caesar urges, shows the Senate a different solution.

"Placet igitur eōs dīmittī et augērī exercitum Catilīnae? Minumē. Sed ita cēnseō: pūblicandās eōrum pecūniās, ipsōs in vinculīs habendōs per mūnicipia quae maxumē opibus valent, neu quis dē eīs posteā ad senātum
295 referat nēve cum populō agat; quī aliter fēcerit, senātum exīstumāre eum contrā rem pūblicam et salūtem omnium factūrum."

1. **For what two reasons does Caesar suggest that whipping is not appropriate?** (280–282)
2. **Why does Caesar not agree with the death penalty?** (286–287)
3. **What new, far-reaching consideration does Caesar introduce into the debate in line 289?**
4. **List the four specific stipulations Caesar lays down in his *sententia*.** (293–296)

297 **ūnam . . . alteram** (298): in apposition to **duās . . . sententiās. eōs . . . esse multandōs** (298): indirect statement completing **cēnset.**

298 **haec:** "all this." In contexts of this sort, an orator frequently uses **haec** (*n pl*) to signify the state as a whole, represented by the panorama of Rome's center of government, the Forum. This figure is called synecdoche. Doubtless the demonstrative is uttered with a sweeping gesture designed to call attention to the immediate surroundings as symbolic of Rome's greatness. **multō** (1), to punish. **quī:** subject of both **removet** (299) and **amplectitur** (300); notice the asyndeton.

299 ***removeō, removēre** (2), **remōvī, remōtum**, to remove. **acerbitās, acerbitātis** (*f*), bitterness, harshness. **acerbitātēs:** concrete plural.

300 **amplector, amplectī** (3), **amplexus sum**, to embrace, (metaphorically) espouse. ***dignitās, dignitātis** (*f*), prestige, merit, worth. **in summā sevēritāte versātur:** "is indulging in the highest degree of strictness."

301 **Alter eōs, quī . . . oportēre** (303): **alter** is subject of **nōn putat** (303), which is completed by **oportēre** (303), an infinitive of an impersonal verb forming an indirect statement; **oportēre**, in turn, governs the indirect statement **eōs** (301) **. . . fruī** (+ ablative) **vītā . . . spīritū** (303). **prīvāre . . . exstinguere** (302): each of the three infinitives is complementary, going with **cōnātī sunt**, expressed in the first clause only.

303 **pūnctus, -ūs** (*m*), point. **pūnctum temporis:** accusative of duration of time, "for even an instant."

305 **ūsūrpō** (1) (+ **in** + *acc.*), to apply to, employ or use (something) on or against. **recordor, recordārī** (1), **recordātus sum**, to remember, keep in mind. **mortem:** accusative subject of **esse . . . cōnstitūtam** (306), indirect statement completing **intellegit. dīs:** = **deīs**, a common contraction.

306 **necessitātem . . . quiētem** (307): predicate complements with **esse . . . constitūtam**, "as either . . . or. . . ." **aut . . . aut:** notice the chiastic order in the placing of the accusatives and their respective dependent genitives (**nātūrae** and **labōrum ac miseriārum**).

307 **eam:** = **mortem. invītī . . . libenter** (308): frequently an author may use an adjective such as **invītī** parallel with an adverb because the adjective can have adverbial force.

308 **oppetō, oppetere** (3), **oppetīvī, oppetītum**, to go to meet. ***vērō**, but in fact. Postpositives such as **vērō, autem, enim**, and (usually) **igitur** cannot stand first in the clause. **sempiternus, -a, -um**, everlasting, never-ending. **ad . . . poenam:** "to serve as punishment" (**ad** + accusative frequently expresses purpose).

309 **singulāris, -is, -e**, unique, unprecedented. **inventa sunt:** "have now been found," present perfect to contrast with the ways of the past. **dispertiō** (4), to distribute. Cicero is brief: (**eōs**) (i.e., the men in custody) **dispertīrī iubet**, "he (Caesar) orders (them) to be distributed among. . . . " Thus **mūnicipiīs** is dative, in sense equivalent to **per mūnicipia.** ***mūnicipium, -ī** (*n*), self-governing town in Italy possessing Roman citizenship.

311 **inīquitās, inīquitātis** (*f*), unfairness, injustice. **sī . . . velīs:** future less vivid condition, "if you were to decide."

312 **dēcernātur:** what use of the subjunctive?

313 **reperiam, quī:** understood is **eōs** as the object of **reperiam** and antecedent of **quī**, which is the subject of **nōn putent**, a characteristic subjunctive. **esse suae dignitātis recūsāre: esse**, an infinitive in indirect discourse governed by **putent**, has as its predicate the characteristic genitive **suae dignitātis**, "that it is in keeping with their merit." The substantive infinitive **recūsāre** serves as the subject of the indirect statement and has **id** and its modifier, **quod . . . statueritis**, as its object; translate, "to refuse what you decide." The verb **statueritis** is perfect subjunctive because the **quod** clause is subordinate to the indirect statement.

314 **adiungō, adiungere** (3), **adiūnxī, adiūnctum**, to subjoin, add on. The subject is **Caesar.**

315 **eōrum:** "of the conspirators"; **eōrum** should probably be construed with **vincula** rather than with **quis. rūperit:** perfect subjunctive representing (in primary sequence) in virtual indirect discourse the terms of Caesar's proposal, which would have been expressed in the future perfect indicative: "If anyone breaks these men loose (**rūperit**, future perfect), the **municipium** will pay a penalty." **horribilis, -is, -e**, fearful, dreadful. **horribilīs:** connected by **et** to **dignās.**

Caesar's view won adherents among the next several speakers, so that other senators and even Silanus himself backed away from the proposal to execute the prisoners. As president of the meeting, the consul Cicero focuses all the previous speakers' **sententiae** *into two basic and conflicting viewpoints so as to help the senators see the main issues clearly.*

[7.] "Videō duās adhūc esse sententiās, ūnam D. Sīlānī, quī cēnset eōs, quī haec dēlēre cōnātī sunt, morte esse multandōs, alteram C. Caesaris, quī mortis poenam removet, cēterōrum suppliciōrum omnīs acerbitātēs

300 amplectitur. Uterque et prō suā dignitāte et prō rērum magnitūdine in summā sevēritāte versātur. Alter eōs, quī nōs omnīs vītā prīvāre cōnātī sunt, quī dēlēre imperium, quī populī Rōmānī nōmen exstinguere, pūnctum temporis fruī vītā et hōc commūnī spīritū nōn putat oportēre, atque hoc genus poenae saepe in improbōs cīvīs in hāc rē pūblicā esse

305 ūsūrpātum recordātur. Alter intellegit mortem ab dīs immortālibus nōn esse supplicī causā cōnstitūtam, sed aut necessitātem nātūrae aut labōrum ac miseriārum quiētem. Itaque eam sapientēs numquam invītī, fortēs saepe etiam libenter oppetīvērunt. Vincula vērō et ea sempiterna certē ad singulārem poenam nefāriī sceleris inventa sunt. Mūnicipiīs dispertīrī

310 iubet.

Cicero expresses his own misgivings over Caesar's proposal, but agrees to follow the Senate's direction, whatever it decides.

"Habēre vidētur ista rēs inīquitātem sī imperāre velīs, difficultātem sī rogāre: dēcernātur tamen, sī placet. [8.] Ego enim suscipiam, et, ut spērō, reperiam, quī id, quod salūtis omnium causā statueritis, nōn putent esse suae dignitātis recūsāre. Adiungit gravem poenam mūnicipiīs, sī quis

315 eōrum vincula rūperit: horribilīs custōdiās circumdat et dignās scelere hominum perditōrum.

1. What is the purpose of Cicero's opening sentence? (297–300)
2. What, according to Cicero, have both Silanus and Caesar endeavored to do? (300–301)
3. What are the three crimes that we learn Silanus accused the conspirators of committing? (301–302)
4. Why would it be unjust or unfair for the Senate to command the Italian *mūnicipia* to support the conspirators for life? (311–312) Why would it be awkward to ask it of them as friends?
5. What does Cicero promise to do, and what warnings does he offer the Senate before it votes? (312–314)
6. What is it in Caesar's proposal that would make the imprisonment *horribilis*? (314–315)

317 **sīve . . . sīve** (318): "if on the one hand . . . ; but if. . . . " **hoc**: i.e., Caesar's
sententia. **comitem**: when the Senate has voted, Cicero will be able to take news
of Caesar's support with him when he goes out to inform the people, through a
contiō, of the Senate's decision.

318 **populō**: dative with **cārum atque iūcundum**. We may take Cicero to mean that the
people will support the Senate if it adopts Caesar's proposal because Caesar is
popular with the people.

319 **vituperātiō, vituperātiōnis** (*f*), blame. The ablative is one of separation with **exsolvet**
(320).

320 **exsolvō, exsolvere** (3), **exsolvī, exsolūtum**, to release. Remember that the people by
now would be easy to inflame against Catiline because of the real threat of civil
war, and so would be ready to follow Silanus' call for the death penalty if the
Senate chose to adopt his proposal. **obtineō, obtinēre** (2), **obtinuī, obtentum**,
(here) to maintain, prove. **eam**: i.e., (Silanus') **sententiam**, subject of **fuisse** in an
indirect statement. **Quamquam**: "And yet" (as frequently in Cicero).

321 **quae**: the interrogative adjective modifying **crūdēlitās** (322), subject of **potest**.
in . . . immānitāte pūniendā: "in punishing . . . " **immānitās, immānitātis** (*f*),
enormity, monstrousness.

322 **sēnsus, -ūs** (*m*), feeling. **ita mihi . . . liceat, ut ego** (323) . . . **moveor** (324): formula
for a wish, "so may I enjoy . . . , as I am moved. . . . "

323 **liceat**: optative subjunctive. **perfruor, perfruī** (3), **perfructus sum** (+ *abl.*), to enjoy
fully. **quod**: "(I say this) because." **causā**: "case," a legal usage that we have
adopted in the English "show just cause." **vehementior**: the comparative here
suggests "more than is usual," i.e., "rather."

324 **atrōcitās, atrōcitātis** (*f*), savagery. **animus**: not only "mind" but what is in the
mind, therefore (as here) "intent." **mītis, -is, -e**, mild, easygoing.

326 **Quae cum ita sint**: "Given this state of affairs." Cicero broadens his style in the
peroration, leaving behind the precise arguments of his earlier lines. **prō**: "in
place of." This long series of parallel phrases ends with **dīligentiā** (332). **quam
neglēxī**: when Cicero renounced his right to govern a province, he gave up the
imperium he would have exercised as proconsul in 62, the prospect of a military
command (**exercitus**) while governor of his province, and the possibility of being
allowed to celebrate a triumph (**triumphus**, 327) on his return to Rome in recognition of his accomplishments as a military commander. The **triumphus** was a
public holiday, paid for with public funds on authority of the Senate, and granted
to celebrate a significant victory in the field for which the **dux** had been ac-
claimed by his army as **imperātor**.

328 **clientēla, -ae** (*f*), connections of loyalty with clients (dependents). Cicero, if he had
not declined his appointment as governor for the following year, would have stood
to gain potentially useful ties with the important families in his province.
hospitium, -ī (*n*), ties of friendship (between persons of different states).

329 **urbānus, -a, -um**, characteristic of a city. **urbānīs opibus**: "by such influence (**opēs**)
as my [activities in my] city afford me." Cicero claims that he looks after (**tueor**)
the ties he enjoys with various provincials (**quae** = **clientēlās** and **hospitia**) with
no less effort (**nōn minōre labōre**, ablative of manner) than (**quam**) that with
which he acquires (**comparō**) such relationships.

330 ***prō meīs . . . prōque** (331): **prō** here means "in exchange for."

331 ***cōnservō** (1), to preserve. **ad cōnservandam**: a formula expressing purpose, "to. . . ."

332 **dīligentia, -ae** (*f*), painstaking care. **nihil**: accusative, object of **postulō** (333).

333 **quae dum erit . . . fīxa**: "as long as it (i.e., **memoria meī cōnsulātūs**) shall remain
secure."

334 **saepiō, saepīre** (4), **saepsī, saeptum**, to hedge, encircle. **quodsī**, but if. Like **sī**,
quodsī may introduce a future more vivid condition.

336 **satis erit praesidī**: the subject of **erit** is **satis** + the partitive genitive; **cui** (335) is
dative of possession: "who will surely have adequate protection." This clause
forms the apodosis of the clause **sī . . . mēmineritis** (337–338). Cicero's son was
born two years earlier. **ad**: "for"; see note to line 308 above.

337 **sī . . . mēmineritis** (338): i.e., **sī mēmineritis illum esse fīlium eius quī. . . .**
suō sōlīus perīculō: the genitive of **sōlus** (adjective for noun) is possessive,
reinforcing the reflexive adjective **suus**; this structure is impossible to duplicate in
English but is approximated with "at danger to himself alone." The use of **sōlus**
creates a stronger contrast with **haec omnia**. **cōnservārit**: = **cōnservāverit**. Why
perfect subjunctive?

50

Cicero makes it clear to the Senate that he does not favor Caesar's proposal, and it is obvious that he would like the Senate to sanction the death penalty. Nonetheless, he says, "Whether you vote for Silanus' viewpoint or Caesar's, I am prepared to defend your choice before the people. Still, where would the real cruelty lie: in punishing conspirators or in putting the citizens in danger of their lives?"

[11.] "Quam ob rem sīve hoc statueritis, dederitis mihi comitem ad cōntiōnem populō cārum atque iūcundum; sīve Sīlānī sententiam sequī mālueritis, facile mē atque vōs crūdēlitātis vituperātiōne populus Rōmānus
320 exsolvet, atque obtinēbō eam multō lēniōrem fuisse. Quamquam, patrēs cōnscrīptī, quae potest esse in tantī sceleris immānitāte pūniendā crūdēlitās? Ego enim dē meō sēnsū iūdicō. Nam ita mihi salvā rē pūblicā vōbīscum perfruī liceat, ut ego—quod in hāc causā vehementior sum—nōn atrōcitāte animī moveor (quis enim est mē mītior?) sed singulārī quādam
325 hūmānitāte et misericordiā.

*Cicero next painted for the Senate a vivid picture of Lentulus ruling as king, and of the others lording it over a vanquished city. He reassured the Senate that all classes in Rome would support the death penalty: **equitēs**, civil servants, shopkeepers, freedmen, and even the slaves. The Senate should take advantage of this **concordia**. For himself, Cicero will never regret taking the firmest measures now. In his peroration, Cicero concludes with a magnificent declaration of his devotion to Rome and his willingness to sacrifice all but his son to save the state.*

[23.] "Quae cum ita sint, prō imperiō, prō exercitū, prō prōvinciā quam neglēxī, prō triumphō cēterīsque laudis īnsignibus quae sunt ā mē propter urbis vestraeque salūtis custōdiam repudiāta, prō clientēlīs hospitiīsque prōvinciālibus (quae tamen urbānīs opibus nōn minōre labōre tueor quam
330 comparō), prō hīs igitur omnibus rēbus, prō meīs in vōs singulāribus studiīs prōque hāc, quam perspicitis, ad cōnservandam rem pūblicam dīligentiā, nihil ā vōbīs nisi huius temporis tōtīusque meī cōnsulātūs memoriam postulō: quae dum erit in vestrīs fīxa mentibus, tūtissimō mē mūrō saeptum esse arbitrābor. Quodsī meam spem vīs improbōrum
335 fefellerit atque superāverit, commendō vōbīs parvum meum fīlium, cui profectō satis erit praesidī nōn sōlum ad salūtem, vērum etiam ad dignitātem, sī eius, quī haec omnia suō sōlīus perīculō cōnservārit, illum fīlium esse mēmineritis.

1. Why does Cicero claim that the punishment proposed by Silanus is *multō lēnior?* (320)
2. What is the effect of juxtaposing *immānitāte* with the adjective *tantī?* (321)
3. Why does Cicero postpone the subject *crūdēlitās* to the end of the sentence? (320–322)
4. By what stylistic means does Cicero hint at which of the two significant opinions he himself preferred? (320–322)
5. What is the purpose of Cicero's rhetorical question *quis enim est mē mītior?* (324)
6. What is the effect on the audience of the climax developed in lines 326–333?
7. What does the litotes *nōn minōre* (329) really mean? Why is this figure useful here?
8. Why does Cicero mention his son? (335–338)

339 **quāpropter**, on which account, therefore. **salūte . . . rē pūblicā** (342): this long series of nouns, while sounding like a string of platitudes, in fact picks up all those interests of the senators that Cicero had spent much time in his speech outlining severally and in some detail. **vestrā populīque Rōmānī**: here the possessive adjective is coordinated with the possessive genitive of a noun; see note on line 337 above.

340 ***focus, -ī** (m), hearth. **focīs**: here by synecdoche representing the home.

342 **dēcernite dīligenter**: the hammer-blows of the anaphora **dē . . . dē** (339–341) are echoed and rivaled by this deliberate alliteration. For the full effect intended by Cicero, read the whole sentence aloud.

343 **eum cōnsulem, quī**: "a man for your consul who . . ." Account for the subjunctive verbs **dubitet** and **possit** (344). **parēre**: complementary infinitive with **nōn dubitet** ("not to hesitate"). **dēcrētum, -ī** (n), decree.

344 **vīvet**: this future is best translated into the English present tense.

345 **Longē . . . alia**: "quite different"; on **mēns**, see note on **animus**, line 324 above. **rēs atque perīcula** (acc.): hendiadys for "dangerous situation."

346 **nōnnūllī, -ōrum** (m pl), some, a few. The adjective is here used as a noun. **reputō** (1), to reconsider, think back over.

347 **mihi**: take with **videntur. disseruisse**: "to have given us a philosophical lecture." **ārīs atque focīs**: notice that Cicero had used the same cliché (340).

348 **cavēre . . . cōnsultāre** (349): complementary infinitives with **monet** rather than the usual indirect command (**ut** + subjunctive) of classical style. **cavēre** (+ **ab** + abl.), to be on one's guard against.

349 **quid . . . statuāmus**: completing **cōnsultāre**. Identify the subjunctive used in **statuāmus. in illōs**: "against them." **maleficium, -ī** (n), wickedness, offense, crime. **tum . . . ubi** (350): = **tum . . . cum**.

350 **persequāre**: = **persequāris**, potential subjunctive. **nisi prōvīderis**: (here) "haven't prevented"; potential subjunctive (perfect tense). **nē accidat**: negative purpose clause. **frūstrā**: take with **implōrēs**, a potential subjunctive.

351 **implōrō** (1), to appeal to. **captā urbe**: translate as a temporal clause. **nihil . . . relicuī**: lit., "nothing of a remainder" (partitive genitive of **relicuum, -ī**, n); translate, "nothing remains." **relicuī**: = **reliquī** (as in 226). **victīs**: dative, "for those who lose," participle used in place of a noun.

352 **composītē**, in a skillful manner. ***ōrdō, ōrdinis** (m), order, class. Translate here as "this assembly." By metonymy, **ōrdō** commonly means the Senate.

353 **crēdō**: parenthetical, not affecting the grammar of the sentence but qualifying **exīstumāns. falsa . . . memorantur**: the adjective **falsa** supplies the predicate accusative of the participle **exīstumāns** and agrees with **ea**, the antecedent of **quae. ea**: i.e., "stories." **dīvorsō itinere**: "by (taking) a different path," completed with **ā bonīs** (354).

354 **malōs . . . habēre**: indirect statement standing in apposition to **ea**; **malōs** and **bonīs** are masculine used as common gender. **incultus, -a, -um**, neglected, dilapidated. **formīdulōsus, -a, -um**, terrifying. Notice the alliteration, **foeda atque formīdulōsa**. Read the sentence aloud. What effect does this alliteration seem to have?

355 **Itaque**: i.e., in consequence of the view expressed by the words **falsa exīstumāns** (353). **pūblicandās . . . habendōs** (356): supply **esse**.

356 **sint**: = **maneant** or **teneantur**.

357 **condūcō, condūcere** (3), **condūxī, conductum**, to hire. **ēripiantur**: "be abducted," "be rescued," subjunctive in a clause of fearing with **timēns** (356). **quasi . . . sint** (358): "as if there were. . . .," present subjunctive in a conditional clause of comparison in primary sequence.

359 **ibi**: completed by **ubi. plūs possit**: "were (not) capable of more." **Possum** may be used with no completing infinitive but rather with a cognate accusative, on which see note on **nihil valet** above (267). **dēfendere** is here used in an absolute sense without a direct object, = "to offer a defense" (understand "against acts of daring"). **minōres**: for the translation, see the note on **vehementior** (323).

Cicero concludes by reminding the Senate what is at stake and by pledging his steadfast loyalty to its decision.

[24.] "Quāpropter dē summā salūte vestrā populīque Rōmānī, dē vestrīs
340 coniugibus ac līberīs, dē ārīs ac focīs, dē fānīs atque templīs, dē tōtīus
urbis tēctīs ac sēdibus, dē imperiō ac lībertāte, dē salūte Italiae, dē
ūniversā rē pūblicā dēcernite dīligenter, ut īnstituistis, ac fortiter. Habētis
eum cōnsulem, quī et pārēre vestrīs dēcrētīs nōn dubitet et ea, quae
statueritis, quoad vīvet, dēfendere et per sē ipsum praestāre possit."

RESUMPTION OF SALLUST'S *BELLUM CATILINAE*

*The tribune-elect Cato, a strict republican, has noticed that the Senate
has begun to waver because of Caesar's speech. When his turn to speak
comes, he rises to warn that this problem is not like others that the
Senate has faced in the past.*

345 [52.] "Longē mihi alia mēns est, patrēs cōnscrīptī, cum rēs atque perīcula
nostra cōnsīderō et cum sententiās nōnnūllōrum ipse mēcum reputō. Illī
mihi disseruisse videntur dē poenā eōrum quī patriae, parentibus, ārīs
atque focīs suīs bellum parāvēre; rēs autem monet cavēre ab illīs magis
quam quid in illōs statuāmus cōnsultāre. Nam cētera maleficia tum
350 persequāre ubi facta sunt; hoc nisi prōvīderis nē accidat, ubi ēvēnit frūstrā
iūdicia implōrēs: captā urbe nihil fit relicuī victīs.

*Cato cynically and scathingly tells the Senate to think of their treasured
wealth, if the institutions of the state mean nothing to them. If Catiline
prevails, "all that we own, however we regard it," will be stolen. After
warning that it is the survival of the citizen body that hangs in the bal-
ance, Cato mockingly derides Caesar's fastidiousness over executing the
prisoners.*

"Bene et compositē C. Caesar paulō ante in hōc ōrdine dē vītā et morte
disseruit, crēdō, falsa exīstumāns ea quae dē īnferīs memorantur, dīvorsō
itinere malōs ā bonīs loca taetra, inculta, foeda atque formīdulōsa habēre.
355 Itaque cēnsuit pecūniās eōrum pūblicandās, ipsōs per mūnicipia in
custōdiīs habendōs, vidēlicet timēns nē, sī Rōmae sint, aut ā populāribus
coniūrātiōnis aut ā multitūdine conductā per vim ēripiantur: quasi vērō
malī atque scelestī tantummodo in urbe et nōn per tōtam Italiam sint, aut
nōn ibi plūs possit audācia ubi ad dēfendundum opēs minōrēs sunt.

1. In what sense are there both a contrast and a parallelism between the sentences,
    Quāpropter . . . fortiter (339–342) and *Quodsī . . . memineritis* (334–338)?
2. In what ways does the sentence *Habētis . . . possit* (342–344) serve to sum up all
    that Cicero has said to the Senate in this speech? What points does it not
    include?
3. What is Cato making clear in the anaphora *mihi . . . ipse mēcum . . . mihi*?
    (345–347)
4. What fundamental difference does Cato perceive between the crime being dis-
    cussed here and all other crimes? (349–351)
5. Explain the epigram, *captā urbe nihil fit relicuī victīs.* (351)
6. What effect does the alliteration *foeda atque formīdulōsa* have? (354) (*Hint:* read
    the sentence aloud.)
7. With what warning does Cato condemn Caesar's view? (357–359)

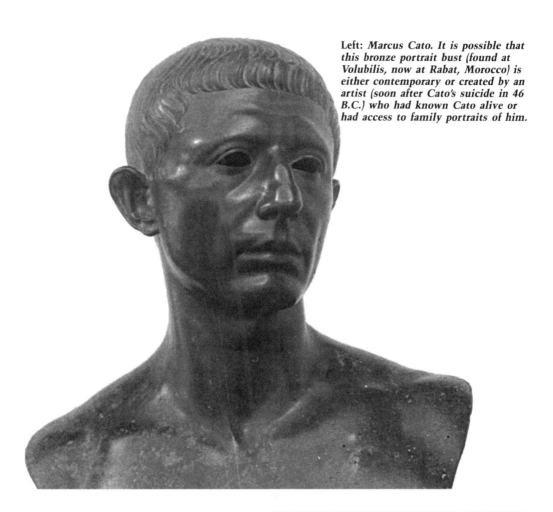

Left: *Marcus Cato. It is possible that this bronze portrait bust (found at Volubilis, now at Rabat, Morocco) is either contemporary or created by an artist (soon after Cato's suicide in 46 B.C.) who had known Cato alive or had access to family portraits of him.*

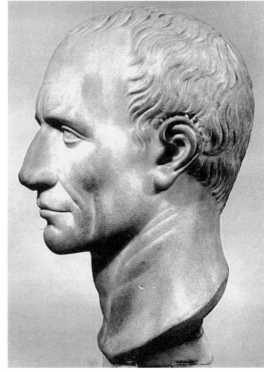

Right: *Julius Caesar. It is only from contemporary coins that we can guess what Caesar really looked like. This marble bust in the British Museum conforms with the numismatic evidence better than most and certainly catches the character of Caesar that we receive from history.*

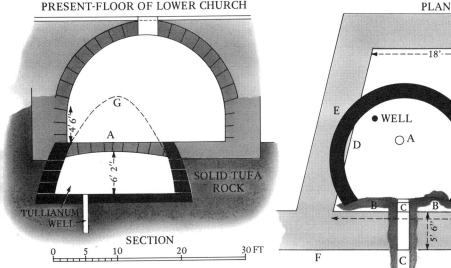

PRESENT-FLOOR OF LOWER CHURCH

PLAN

SECTION

TULLIÅNUM WELL

SOLID TUFA ROCK

0   5   10   20   30 FT

18'

25'

26'

5' 6'

● WELL

E

D

A

B   C   B

C

F   C   F

G

A

4' 6"

6' 2"

Above: *Mamertine Prison, section and plan. A: opening in floor over Tulliānum (the only access to it). BB: solid tufa rock. CC: branch of the cloāca or sewer. DE: location of modern stairs and door. FF: front wall of prison with inscription recording its restoration by the suffect consuls of ca. A.D. 39–42 on order of the Senate. G: probable original top of the Tulliānum.*

Above: Carcer. *This is the upper and later chamber of the prison. It was used to detain prisoners awaiting trial or execution. Because of martyrdoms, it was later turned into a Christian shrine; the altar and plaque are more recent additions.*

Tulliānum. *This was the dreaded lower chamber where executions took place. A channel in the rock gave access to the main sewer of Rome, which came down through the center of the Forum.*

55

360 *quāre, therefore. vānus, -a, -um, empty, vain. Cato puts very early in the sentence the *epithet* with which he chooses to characterize Caesar's proposal: "lacking solid plausibility" might catch the metaphor. Against this emptiness Cato immediately contrasts such "solid" considerations as Catiline's menacing army (363). metuō, metuere (3), metuī, metūtum, to fear, dread. Caesar is subject of metuit and timet (361).

361 eō magis: "all the more." mē ... timēre (362): indirect statement completing rēfert (impersonal), "it is important (that). . . ." mihi atque vōbīs: dative of interest with timēre.

362 prō certō habēre, to be certain. Completed with an indirect statement, vōs ... dēcernere (363–364).

363 habētōte: plural of the future imperative; use the regular English present imperative.

364 Quantō ... tantō: "the more ... the more." The ablatives of degree of difference go with the comparatives attentius and īnfirmior. vōs ... illīs ... vōs (365) ... omnēs: Sallust uses these paired and contrasted pronouns in symmetry to set up a clear antithesis. This use of rhetorical devices makes the argument of the sentence highly persuasive. Cato is made to give it a sense of rational logic that does not feed into Caesar's charge of emotionalism. attentē, attentively, carefully. ea: neuter plural referring generally to the concerns outlined in the previous sentence. illīs animus ... erit: "their spirit will be. . . ." To whom does illīs refer?

365 paululum modo: "even a little," modifying languēre. langueō, languēre (2), languī, to be weak, inactive, feeble. vōs languēre: indirect statement with vīderint. ferōcēs: predicate nominative, "with intent to kill."

366 Quārē ... sūmundum (370): in his peroration, Cato states his proposal (compare the peroration of Caesar, lines 292–296). At the conclusion of the debate, the presiding magistrate puts to a vote in the Senate the proposal that he feels best represents the view of the majority. What meaning of cum suits best with vēnerit (367)?

367 eī: the pronoun refers to the conspirators under arrest.

368 cōnfiteor, cōnfitērī (2), cōnfessus sum, to admit, confess. sē ... parāvisse (369): the grammatical object is caedem ... atque crūdēlia facinora (369).

369 dē cōnfessīs: take with supplicium sūmundum [esse] (370), "those who have confessed should be punished." This indirect statement is object of cēnseō (366).

370 manufestīs rērum capitālium: "those caught red-handed (+ genitive) in capital offenses." maiōrēs, maiōrum (*m pl*), ancestors. mōre maiōrum supplicium sūmundum: the alliteration creates an effect of deliberateness.

371 in ... discessit: the idiom discēdere in (+ accusative) indicates the process of voting by division; it is called discessiō. optumum factū: "best to do," using the supine (in the ablative of respect); the neuter optumum modifies the infinitive antecapere (372), which supplies the object of the participle ratus.

372 *reor, rērī (2), ratus sum, to think. Perfect participles of deponent verbs often have a present sense; thus ratus means "having thought" and therefore "(now) thinking." novō (1), to start afresh. nē quid ... novārētur: "to head off any new attempt." Identify the use of the subjunctive in novārētur.

373 trēsvirī, trēsvirōrum (*m pl*), three joint commissioners, a Board of Three. The trēsvirī capitālēs were lower magistrates in charge of supervising executions and related concerns. trēsvirōs ... parāre: accusative and objective infinitive with iubet. quae: accusative plural, object of postulābat, the subject of which is supplicium.

374 Lentulum ... dēdūcit: try to imagine how gravely observers would have regarded the sight of their consul personally escorting the ex-praetor Lentulus to his execution. carcerem: Sallust means the so-called Mamertine Prison in the Forum, situated between the Temple of Concord and the Senate House (Curia Hostilia); see plan, p. 6. The carcer had an upper chamber for detaining prisoners and an underground chamber, the Tulliānum, where executions were carried out. The Tulliānum is undoubtedly one of the oldest structures remaining from Republican Rome. While tradition ascribed its foundation to various kings, the name has also been related to tullus, an Oscan word for spring or well. The origin of the name Mamertine is obscure. It was never used to identify this building in ancient times but may in fact be derived from the name of an owner of the land in medieval times. cēterīs: dative.

*"Why be afraid of five prisoners? Fear rather a hostile army on the loose.
Or is Caesar alone not afraid of that while all the rest of us are? And
why is he not?"* Cato warns that only decisive action will show Catiline's
army what awaits those who have attacked Rome. Hesitation now means
destruction.

360 "Quārē vānum equidem hoc cōnsilium est, sī perīculum ex illīs metuit; sī
in tantō omnium metū sōlus nōn timet, eō magis rēfert mē mihi atque
vōbīs timēre. Quārē cum dē P. Lentulō cēterīsque statuētis, prō certō
habētōte vōs simul dē exercitū Catilīnae et dē omnibus coniūrātīs
dēcernere. Quantō vōs attentius ea agētis, tantō illīs animus īnfirmior erit;
365 sī paululum modo vōs languēre vīderint, iam omnēs ferōcēs aderunt.

*In a long passage not quoted here, Cato hurls stinging criticism at the
senators for their failure to safeguard the national interests. He accuses
them of hypocrisy and of being too timid to defend moral values that
formerly insured efficiency of rule and justice in the provinces. They have
lost independence of spirit and deal only for selfish advantage. The ruling
class does not honor Rome's best men, but allows ambition to win out
over merit. They are slaves to money, pleasure, and influence. Some of
them even sacrifice their country, even strive to destroy it themselves. We
do not deserve the help of the gods, Cato asserts, when we cannot help
ourselves. Not so was Rome's glory won. Why spare men the shame of
death by execution who have spared themselves no other shame? Furthermore, while we argue, they are learning all our plans.*

"Quārē ego ita cēnseō: cum nefāriō cōnsiliō scelerātōrum cīvium rēs
pūblica in maxuma perīcula vēnerit, eīque indiciō T. Volturcī et lēgātōrum
Allobrogum convictī cōnfessīque sint caedem, incendia, aliaque sē foeda
atque crūdēlia facinora in cīvīs patriamque parāvisse, dē cōnfessīs, sīcutī
370 dē manufestīs rērum capitālium, mōre maiōrum supplicium sūmundum."

*Ashamed that they should be branded self-interested cowards, the Senate
overwhelmingly adopted Cato's proposal as a* **senātūs cōnsultum**. *Cicero
lost no time in carrying out the Senate's policy, since night was approach-
ing and might otherwise hold unexpected dangers for the city.*

[55.] Postquam senātus in Catōnis sententiam discessit, cōnsul optumum
factū ratus noctem quae īnstābat antecapere nē quid eō spatiō novārētur,
trēsvirōs quae supplicium postulābat parāre iubet; ipse, praesidiīs
dispositīs, Lentulum in carcerem dēdūcit; idem fit cēterīs per praetōrēs.

1. **What epithet does Cato use to characterize Caesar's proposal?** (360)
2. **Because of the strong antithesis between *omnium* and *sōlus* (361), what insinua-
tion against Caesar's loyalty may Cato have intended us to see in the idea, *eō
magis rēfert mē . . . timēre* (361–362)?**
3. **According to Cato, what broader significance will the Senate's decision about the
conspirators have?** (364–365)
4. **What moral contrast is Cato setting up by using *languēre* and *ferōcēs*?** (365)
5. **Name the rhetorical figure used in the words *rēs pūblica vēnerit*.** (366–367)
6. **What four moves did the consul Cicero make just before nightfall?** (373–374)
How does Sallust convey to the reader the speed with which he moved?

375 **ubi . . . ascenderis**: "when you go up," 2nd person general (perfect subjunctive of a potential act regarded as completed). To a pedestrian leaving the Forum, the **carcer** was approached by climbing a gentle rise, with the **Cūria** on the right and on the left the Temple of Concord with, behind that, the northern mound of the **Arx**. (See plans, pp. 5, 6) The prison itself was an old well-house that had been overlaid by more recent urban development. The prison would be **ad laevam** (376) to one headed between the Capitol and the Quirinal Hill.

376 **laeva, -ae** (*f*), the left hand, left-hand side, left. Notice throughout this passage (375–378) how much attention Sallust pays to commonplace, realistic descriptive detail. This brings the reader into the setting and the story. **duodecim pedēs**: accusative of extent, with **dēpressus**. **dēprimō, dēprimere** (3), **dēpressī, dēpressum**, to sink. **dēpressus**: "sunk deep," modifying **locus**. **Eum**: i.e., **locum**; so **eius** (378) means "its."

377 **īnsuper**, above, overhead. **camera, -ae** (*f*), vault. Compare Sallust's details with those in the picture on page 55. **fornix, fornicis** (*m*), arch. **lapideīs fornicibus iūncta**: "roofed over with arches of stone."

378 **incultus, -ūs** (*m*), neglect. **incultū, tenebrīs, odōre**: causal ablatives explaining **foeda atque terribilis**. The asyndeton creates a stark effect. **In eum locum**: placed first to bridge the two sentences and return us to the story.

379 **vindicēs rērum capitālium**: "executioners," under the supervision of the **trēsvirī**. **quibus**: dative with the compound verb **praeceptum erat** (380).

380 **praeceptum erat** (*impersonal*): "instructions had been given." **laqueus, -ī** (*m*), noose. **gula -ae** (*f*), throat, neck. Notice the chilling suddenness with which the end arrives. **patricius, -ī** (*m*), a patrician (see note on line 168). There appears to be irony in this reference to the **gēns Cornēlia**, considering how great Lentulus had depicted it to be (238–240) and the shamefulness of his manner of death.

381 **Rōmae**: locative. There is *pathos* in this remark about Lentulus' career.

382 **mōribus factīsque suīs**: ablative explaining **dignum** (381). As praetor of 74 Lentulus supervised a trial in which jurors' votes were bought; the scandal damaged his reputation. This and some misconduct in his consulship of 71 may have led to his expulsion from the Senate by the censors of 70 B.C. As praetor in 63 he was able to return to the Senate by virtue of his office. **Cethēgō, Statiliō, Gabīniō, Caepāriō**: Cethegus had been impatient for political advancement, and his own brother had just voted for his execution. Statilius and Gabinius had been ready to set fires around Rome, while Caeparius' role was to "raise shepherds in Apulia," according to Cicero (*Cat.* III.14). These four rank unquestionably below Lentulus in importance to the conspiracy and so here merit the briefest attention.

*Almost next door to the Temple of Concord lies the precinct of the **carcer**. Beneath this grim prison is the chamber known as the **Tulliānum**, of which Sallust now gives us a stark description. Deep below ground in this black and horrible place, the five arrested conspirators meet their shameful end.*

375   Est in carcere locus, quod Tulliānum appellātur, ubi paululum ascenderis
     ad laevam, circiter duodecim pedēs humī dēpressus. Eum mūniunt
     undique parietēs atque īnsuper camera lapideīs fornicibus iūncta; sed
     incultū, tenebrīs, odōre foeda atque terribilis eius faciēs est. In eum locum
     postquam dēmissus est Lentulus, vindicēs rērum capitālium, quibus
380   praeceptum erat, laqueō gulam frēgēre. Ita ille patricius ex gente
     clārissumā Corneliōrum, quī cōnsulāre imperium Rōmae habuerat, dignum
     mōribus factīsque suīs exitium vītae invēnit. Dē Cethēgō, Statiliō,
     Gabīniō, Caepāriō eōdem modō supplicium sūmptum est.

1. From the poetical and elevated style of rhetoric, Sallust quite suddenly changes to plain prose. Examine the sentence *Est in carcere . . . dēpressus* (375–376), and find evidence for this quality. (Consider such features as word patterns, word sense, lack of rhetorical figures, and subject matter.)
2. What is the effect for the reader of the unexpected switch to the 2nd person singular in *ascenderis*? (375)
3. What details of description make the building unique and unforgettable for the reader? (376–378)
4. How does Sallust create a tone of pathos in his account of Lentulus' death? (380–382)
5. Why does Sallust avoid giving a similar account for each of the other prisoners? (382–383)

384 **cōpiā**: supply **mīlitum**.

385 **addūxerat**: i.e., to the camp in Etruria where his army was mustering. The pluper-
fects throughout this paragraph indicate actions taken *before* the executions in
Rome were carried out. **cohortīs**: accusative. A legion comprised ten cohorts,
and when up to strength numbered about 5,000 infantry. Sallust suggests that
Catiline formed twenty cohorts that were understrength. **prō**: "in proportion to."

386 **compleō, complēre** (2), **complēvī, complētum**, to fill. **ut quisque ... distribuerat**
(387): "as individual volunteers or co-conspirators came ..., he distributed them
... (among his cohorts)."

387 **brevī spatiō (temporis)**: = **mox**. **numerō**: ablative of respect, "as regards the. . . ."
The adequacy of the number of men is contrasted with the fact, stated below,
that three out of every four soldiers lacked regulation arms.

388 **expleō, explēre** (2), **explēvī, explētum**, to fill up, round off (a number). **cum ...
habuisset**: concessive. **initiō**: temporal ablative.

389 **mīlitāris, -is, -e**, of a soldier, a soldier's. Such standard armor included the **gladius,
pīlum, scūtum, lōrīca, cassis** (helmet), and **ocreae** (greaves). See the picture on p. 63.

390 **sparus, -ī** (m), (short) hunting javelin. **lancea, -ae** (f), light spear. Vergil (*Aeneid*
XII.374–375) tells us that it was broad-headed. **praeacūtus, -a, -um**, sharpened at
the front end.

391 **sudis, sudis** (f), stake, post, picket.

*As the December evening closed in, Cicero came out of the **carcer** to meet a crowd assembled in the **comitium** (see plan, p. 6). Uttering his famous **"Vīxērunt"** ("They're dead"), he spoke briefly to assure the people that all would be well. They escorted him home triumphantly by torchlight. Thus ended the conspiracy in Rome. Cicero and Cato had been right: with these executions the supply of conspirators slipping northward to join Catiline's army dried up. The government had finally taken a stand that did real damage to Catiline's revolution.*

Meanwhile, in Etruria Catiline had been building an army, using Manlius' original band of 2,000 and adding new arrivals as they came. By the time of the executions just described, Catiline had managed to form two entire legions, though his men were inadequately armed.

[56.] Dum ea Rōmae geruntur, Catilīna ex omnī cōpiā quam et ipse
385 addūxerat et Mānlius habuerat, duās legiōnēs īnstituit; cohortīs prō
numerō mīlitum complet. Deinde, ut quisque voluntārius aut ex sociīs in
castra vēnerat, aequāliter distribuerat, ac brevī spatiō legiōnēs numerō
hominum explēverat, cum initiō nōn amplius duōbus mīlibus habuisset.
Sed ex omnī cōpiā circiter pars quārta erat mīlitāribus armīs īnstrūcta;
390 cēterī, ut quemque cāsus armāverat, sparōs aut lanceās, aliī praeacūtās
sudīs portābant.

1. **Give a reason why Catiline spread his men so thinly.** (385–386) (A consul's army normally numbered two legions, and we recall that Catiline had already illegally assumed the emblems of consular power; see lines 185–186.)
2. **Describe how Catiline's force was armed.** (389–391) **Estimate whether Catiline could expect them to meet a Roman army in a fair fight.**

The emperor Marcus Aurelius sacrificing amid a crowd of military officers and attendants. Notice several types of military standard and details of body armor. Two figures to the extreme right are blowing slender tubae.

392 **nūntius**: translate as "news" because of the two dependent clauses, **Rōmae** (locative) ... **patefactam** (393) and **dē Lentulō ... supplicium sūmptum** (394).

393 **patefactam ... sūmptum** (394): supply **esse** with both participles to make perfect infinitives.

394 **ad bellum**: construe with **inlexerat** (395). **spēs ... studium** (395): nominatives with **inlexerat**.

395 **novārum rērum**: "revolution." **inliciō, inlicere** (3), **inlexī, inlectum**, to entice, seduce, attract. **dīlābor, dīlābī** (3), **dīlāpsus sum**, to slip away. The Greek historian Dio Cassius reports that Catiline's entire force of 3,000 men died in the battle. How many "slipped away" before? **dīlābuntur ... abdūcit** (396): the historical presents allow the dependent purpose clause **utī ... perfugeret** (396–397) to follow secondary sequence.

396 **asper, aspera, asperum**, rough, harsh. **magnīs itineribus**: "by forced marches." This usually meant leaving their baggage behind (see **expedītōs**, 403). **agrum Pistōriēnsem**: the region around the town of Pistoria (now Pistoia, northwest of Florence); see map, p. 2. Catiline avoided the direct route over the plain because of its proximity to Antonius' army. **eō cōnsiliō utī**: "with this plan, that," "intending to," with **perfugeret** (397).

397 **trāmes, trāmitis** (m), footpath, track. **occultē**, secretly. **perfugiō, perfugere** (3), **perfūgī**, to escape.

398 **agrō Pīcēnō**: the broad region of Picenum lay along the Adriatic coast northeast of Rome. In fact, Celer seems to have held his force just beyond its northern limit at Ariminum in Umbria (see map, p. 2). **praesideō, praesidēre** (2), **praesēdī**, to be in command, stand guard. **ex difficultāte rērum**: "as a result of the awkward situation"; take with **exīstumāns** (399).

399 **eadem ... agitāre**: the indirect statement supplies the object of **exīstumāns. eadem illa**: "the very same course of action," the accusative object of the infinitive **agitāre** and the antecedent of **quae**.

400 **iter**: accusative. What is the antecedent of **eius**? **perfuga, -ae** (m), deserter. **sub ipsīs rādīcibus montium ... quā** (401): "at the foot of the very mountains where." Sallust seems to mean below the northern end of the pass that Catiline intended to use over the Apennines.

401 **illī**: dative, "for Catiline," modified by **properantī. in Galliam**: construe with **properantī**.

402 **utpote quī** (+ *subjunctive*): "considering the fact that he." The contrast is between Antonius' much larger army moving over favorable ground and Catiline's much less encumbered force (**expedītōs**, 403). **locīs aequiōribus**: "by way of more favorable ground."

403 **expedītōs** (i.e., Catiline's forces): "unencumbered" because they were moving without unnecessary baggage. **videt**: historical present.

404 Why does Sallust call the Roman army **hostēs**? **sēsē**: = **sē** (compare 255); accusative subject of **clausum** (**esse**), indirect statement with **videt. in urbe**: what city is meant? **rēs advorsās**: "and that things (his situation) were...." The clauses **rēs advorsās** (**esse**) and **neque ... (esse) spem** (405) also complete **videt**.

405 **fugae ... praesidī**: objective genitives with **spem. praesidī**: "reinforcements," "support." Catiline had been hoping to be sent further recruits by his confederates. **optumum factū ratus ... temptāre** (406): "thinking the best thing to do would be to test" (compare note on 371). **factū**: supine (ablative of respect) qualifying **optumum. in tālī rē**: "in such a crisis."

406 **cōnflīgō, cōnflīgere** (3), **cōnflīxī, cōnflīctum**, to fight.

By the new year Catiline was dodging Antonius' army in a cat-and-mouse game, using the hills beyond Florence as cover while awaiting from Rome the reinforcements that now would never come. To make his situation worse, the news from Rome had a demoralizing effect on the forces with him. Finally Metellus Celer and Antonius move in to force battle. Catiline has to decide whose army it is better for him to take on.

[57.] Sed postquam in castra nūntius pervēnit Rōmae coniūrātiōnem patefactam, dē Lentulō et Cethēgō cēterīsque quōs suprā memorāvī supplicium sūmptum, plērīque, quōs ad bellum spēs rapīnārum aut
395 novārum rērum studium inlēxerat, dīlābuntur; reliucōs Catilīna per montīs asperōs magnīs itineribus in agrum Pistōriēnsem abdūcit, eō cōnsiliō utī per trāmitēs occultē perfugeret in Galliam Trānsalpīnam. At Q. Metellus Celer cum tribus legiōnibus in agrō Pīcēnō praesidēbat, ex difficultāte rērum eadem illa exīstumāns, quae suprā dīximus, Catilīnam agitāre.
400 Igitur, ubi iter eius ex perfugīs cognōvit, castra properē mōvit ac sub ipsīs rādīcibus montium cōnsēdit, quā illī dēscēnsus erat in Galliam properantī. Neque tamen Antōnius procul aberat, utpote quī magnō exercitū locīs aequiōribus expedītōs in fugā sequerētur. Sed Catilīna, postquam videt montibus atque cōpiīs hostium sēsē clausum, in urbe rēs advorsās, neque
405 fugae neque praesidī ūllam spem, optumum factū ratus in tālī rē fortūnam bellī temptāre, statuit cum Antōniō quam prīmum cōnflīgere.

1. **What news arrived at Catiline's camp?** (392–394)
2. **What was the effect of most of this news on Catiline's army?** (394–395)
3. **What did Catiline do after receiving the news from Rome?** (395–397)
4. **What two armies hemmed in Catiline's?** (397–398 and 402)
5. **Describe in your own words the situation Catiline faced because of Metellus' moves.** (400–405)
6. **What was Catiline's relationship with Antonius before the outbreak of the rebellion?**
7. **Why do you think Catiline deliberately chose to attack Antonius' army and not that of Metellus Celer?**

Tombstone of the centurion T. Calidius Severus of legion XV Apollinaris, showing his scale lorica, transverse crested cassis, and ocreae

407 **signa canere**: "the trumpet-calls to sound." Standard military instruments for producing signals audible over the din of battle were two varieties of bronze horn: the straight **tuba** and the curved **cornū**, of which the **lituus** (shaped like a shepherd's crook) was a variation. The players were called **tubicen** and **cornicen**, and **canere** was the standard verb used in our sense of "play," "blow"; here, however, **canere** is absolute (has no object), and **signa** is its subject. **iubet ... dēdūcit ... īnstruit** (407–410): the main verbs in this paragraph are in the vivid, or historical, present but, as usual, set up secondary sequence in the dependent verb **esset** (409). **īnstrūctōs**: into battle formation. Catiline had previously addressed them "at ease" in a speech not included here.

408 **in locum aequom**: "into the plain," leaving behind the natural protection of the hills but enabling more effective warfare by Roman methods. **quō ... animus amplior esset** (409): with a comparative in a purpose clause, **quō** replaces **ut**.

409 **exaequātō perīculō**: those with horses (mostly the officer class, since Catiline appears to have had little or no cavalry) now are made to share the risk equally with the infantry. **exaequō**: = **aequō** (1). **animus**: (here) "resolve" and therefore "determination," "courage." **pedes**: in apposition to **ipse**.

410 **prō locō atque cōpiīs**: i.e., as the site demanded and as his numbers allowed.

411 **pedibus**: ablative of respect, explaining **aeger**. Apparently Antonius was suffering from gout; some historians suggest that this was a pretext to avoid having to attack his former friend. **proeliō**: dative completing **adesse**, "be on hand."

412 **nequeō, nequīre** (*irreg.*), **nequīvī**, to be unable. **lēgātō**: here the military sense is meant, "second-in-command." **Ille**: i.e., Petreius; **ille** frequently marks a change of subject. **cohortīs veterānās ... in fronte, ... cēterum exercitum in subsidiīs** (412–414): note the parallel symmetry.

414 **in subsidiīs**: "in reserve." **circumeō, circumīre** (*irreg.*), **circumiī, circumitum**, to go around. **ūnum quemque**: "each man individually." **nōminō** (1), to address by name.

415 **appellat, hortātur, rogat**: asyndeton. **meminerint**: perfect with present meaning (this verb lacks a present), in primary sequence. Identify the use of the subjunctive in **meminerint**. **sē ... certāre** (416): indirect statement with **meminerint**. The heaping up of **prō** (415–416) by anaphora and asyndeton adds fervor.

417 **explōrātīs**: as a military officer with (according to Sallust) over thirty years' experience, Petreius knows enough to call on reports from scouts and spies (to check his "intelligence reports") before engaging in a conflict whose outcome might have seemed to him predetermined.

418 **incēdō, incēdere** (3), **incessī**, to march, advance. **eō ... unde** (419): lit., "to that place from which," "the point where."

419 **ventum est**: in such a context the impersonal passive is common. **unde ... posset**: relative clause of characteristic. **ferentārius, -ī** (*m*), a skirmisher.

420 **cum īnfestīs signīs**: "with opposing ranks." The word **signa** here is used in the sense of "standards," i.e., (by metonymy) the cohorts identified by their elevated battle colors. **pīla omittunt, gladiīs rēs geritur**: Sallust has stripped away all modifying details to give only essentials. The brisk pace (note the asyndeton) and starkness of style make us see the act of combat in its starkness also.

On 1 January 62 B.C., Cicero and Antonius were replaced as consuls by Silanus and Murena. On or about 5 January, Catiline decided to meet somewhere near Pistoria the army brought against him from Rome by the (now) proconsul Antonius. He first delivered a warm and stirring speech to his men, recalling why they had joined his movement in the first place. He blamed Lentulus' folly and cowardice for the collapse of the conspiracy in Rome. He pointed out that Antonius' army blocked an attack on Rome, and that Metellus Celer's three legions stood in the way of retreat northward into Gaul. Starvation faced Catiline's army if they chose to stay where they were. Only courage leads to freedom: fear would end in betrayal of their cause. Finally he bade them not to die unavenged.

[59.] Catilīna, paululum commorātus, signa canere iubet atque īnstrūctōs ōrdinēs in locum aequom dēdūcit. Dein, remōtīs omnium equīs quō mīlitibus exaequātō perīculō animus amplior esset, ipse pedes exercitum
410 prō locō atque cōpiīs īnstruit.

Protected by mountains on one side and rough, rocky ground on the other, Catiline prepares a narrow but dense front. He keeps slightly more than half his army in reserve. Manlius commands the right wing, and "a man from Fiesole" the left. The proconsul Antonius, in too much pain to lead his army, turns the command over to a seasoned veteran officer, Petreius.

At ex alterā parte C. Antōnius, pedibus aeger, quod proeliō adesse nequībat, M. Petrēiō lēgātō exercitum permittit. Ille cohortīs veterānās, quās tumultūs causā cōnscrīpserat, in fronte, post eās cēterum exercitum in subsidiīs locat. Ipse equō circumiēns ūnum quemque nōmināns
415 appellat, hortātur, rogat ut meminerint sē contrā latrōnēs inermīs prō patriā, prō līberīs, prō ārīs atque focīs suīs certāre.

Taking his time to speak to his men individually, Petreius finally accepts Catiline's challenge. The battle begins with startling suddenness.

[60.] Sed ubi, omnibus rēbus explōrātīs, Petrēius tubā signum dat, cohortīs paulātim incēdere iubet; idem facit hostium exercitus. Postquam eō ventum est unde ā ferentāriīs proelium committī posset, maxumō clāmōre
420 cum īnfestīs signīs concurrunt; pīla omittunt, gladiīs rēs geritur.

1. **After giving his last address (omitted here) to his men, Catiline is described as** *paululum commorātus* **(407). Suggest a reason for this curious detail.**
2. **What did Catiline have done with his officers' horses, and why?** (408–409)
3. **In what position did Catiline himself fight?** (409)
4. **How did Petreius organize his army?** (412–414) **Suggest reasons for this arrangement.**
5. **What is the effect of the asyndeton in line 415?**
6. **For what reasons might Petreius have had his cohorts advance** *paulātim*? (418)

Opposite: Tubae *seen being played during a gladiatorial combat*

Bronze lituus

421 **comminus**, hand-to-hand, at close quarters. **īnstāre**: in narrative, sometimes the infinitive with a subject in the nominative case may be used instead of the imperfect indicative. Other historical infinitives are **versārī**, **succurrere**, **arcessere**, **prōvidēre**, **pugnāre**, and **ferīre** (423–424). This stylistic device, along with the protracted asyndeton, suggests impressionistically the tension, rapidity, and confusion of the battle scene. **illī**: i.e., Catiline's forces; note the rapid change of subject. **haud timidī**: the rhetorical figure litotes pretends to understate the truth and hence draws more attention to the fearlessness of the rebel forces.

422 **resistō, resistere** (3), **restitī**, to stand one's ground. **maxumā vī certātur**: the brevity of style imitates that of **gladiīs rēs geritur** (420).

423 **labōrantibus**: "those who were being hard pressed," dative with **succurrere**. **succurrō, succurrere** (3), **succurrī, succursum** (+ *dat.*), to run to help. **integrōs**: of his twenty cohorts, Catiline had held twelve back in reserve; though, owing to defections, he is left now with only 3,000 of the 10,000 men he had when his army was at its peak. **saucius, -a, -um**, wounded.

424 **multum . . . pugnāre**: cognate accusative (like our "fought a lot"), "fought hard." On this structure, see the note on **nihil valet** (267). Observe the incremental effect of the *climax* in **omnia . . . multum . . . saepe**. **feriō, ferīre** (4), to strike, hit, beat. Notice that **hostem** is singular: Sallust causes our imagination to see each individual enemy soldier that Catiline strikes. **mīlitis et . . . imperātōris officia** (425): these words recall that Catiline had promised to serve his co-conspirators loyally "either as a soldier or as commander" (51–52).

425 **exsequor, exsequī** (3), **exsecūtus sum**, to fulfill.

426 **Petrēius ubi**: by postponing the conjunction, Sallust can use Petreius' name as the connective to switch our attention quickly to the other side of the struggle. **contrā ac ratus erat**: "otherwise than he had anticipated." **tendō, tendere** (3), **tetendī, tentum**, to strive, strain, endeavor.

427 **cohortem praetōriam**: "the commander's cohort," a traditional title dating from the early Republic (when the two heads of state were titled praetors, not consuls), and meaning his bodyguard. **indūcit . . . cōnfoditur** (432): all verbs to the end of this scene are in the vivid present. **indūcō, indūcere** (3), **indūxī, inductum**, to lead into. **eōs**: i.e., **hostīs** (accusative).

428 **alibī**, elsewhere, in other places. **aliōs alibī**: "some in some places, some in others," "in various parts of the battlefield." Compare the idiom **aliī aliōs**. We are to understand that Catiline's army has been split into two bodies so that its force is diminished. **utrimque**, on both sides. **utrimque ex lateribus**, "on both (inner) flanks." Having smashed the enemy's center with a wedge (427), Petreius can direct his own attacking force against the exposed flanks on either side.

429 **Faesulānus**: "the man from Fiesole," possibly P. Furius, who was a Sullan colonist at Faesulae and was still at large on 5 December (see above, line 261). **Catilīna . . . cōnfoditur** (432): the verbs and participles in this sentence are so arranged that strict chronology has been observed, yet the careful adherence to chronology has been achieved through a variety of forms of subordination: **fūsās . . . relicuom** (430, supply **esse** in both clauses) are two indirect statements, one past and one present relative to the verb **videt** (historical present) in the **postquam** clause; **memor** (= "as he remembers," 430) is balanced by the present participle **pugnāns** (432), each serving to qualify the two coordinate main verbs **incurrit** (431) and **cōnfoditur** (432) in the historical present. The structure makes this sentence "periodic."

432 **cōnfodiō, cōnfodere** (3), **cōnfōdī, cōnfossum**, to stab, wound fatally.

433 **tum vērō**: "then indeed." **cernerēs**: "one could perceive," potential subjunctive of past time, generalizing 2nd person.

434 **quem quisque**: **quisque** is postpositive, the subject of **tegēbat** (435).

435 **pugnandō**: ablative of the gerund expressing the same idea as **pugnāns**. **eum**: the demonstrative agrees with **locum**, which is the logical antecedent of **quem** and has been attracted into the relative clause because it is put first.

436 **quōs mediōs**: lit., "whom in the center"; "in the center whom." **disiciō, disicere** (3), **disiēcī, disiectum**, to scatter. **paulō dīvorsius**: "a little farther off."

437 **advorsus, -a, -um**: = adversus. **advorsīs vulneribus**: ablative absolute, "their wounds in the front." **concidō, concidere** (3), **concidī**, to fall, collapse, perish.

438 **paululum** (*diminutive of* **paulum**), just a little, barely. **spīrō** (1), to breathe. **ferōcia, -ae** (f), wildness, indomitability.

439 **retineō, retinēre** (2), **retinuī, retentum**, to keep, retain, hold, preserve.

Sallust depicts the courage, energy, and loyalty to their causes of the warriors on both sides. Catiline's brilliant qualities as a leader of human forces rise to meet the most desperate challenge of his life.

Veterānī, prīstinae virtūtis memorēs, comminus ācriter īnstāre; illī haud timidī resistunt: maxumā vī certātur. Intereā Catilīna cum expedītīs in prīmā aciē versārī, labōrantibus succurrere, integrōs prō sauciīs arcessere, omnia prōvidēre, multum ipse pugnāre, saepe hostem ferīre; strēnuī mīlitis
425 et bonī imperātōris officia simul exsequēbātur.

While Catiline's achievement causes Petreius considerable difficulty and surprise, nonetheless the rebels' comparative weakness is soon evident, and their leader himself falls in the thick of the strife.

Petrēius ubi videt Catilīnam, contrā ac ratus erat, magnā vī tendere, cohortem praetōriam in mediōs hostīs indūcit, eōsque perturbātōs atque aliōs alibī resistentīs interficit; deinde utrimque ex lateribus cēterōs adgreditur. Mānlius et Faesulānus in prīmīs pugnantēs cadunt. Catilīna,
430 postquam fūsās cōpiās sēque cum paucīs relicuom videt, memor generis atque prīstinae suae dignitātis, in cōnfertissumōs hostīs incurrit ibique pugnāns cōnfoditur.

In the aftermath, the valor of the combatants' struggle rises above their torn corpses. Catiline is perceived, defiant in his last breath, surrounded by his dead foes.

[61.] Sed cōnfectō proeliō, tum vērō cernerēs quanta audācia quantaque animī vīs fuisset in exercitū Catilīnae. Nam ferē quem quisque vīvos
435 pugnandō locum cēperat, eum āmissā animā corpore tegēbat. Paucī autem, quōs mediōs cohors praetōria disiēcerat, paulō dīvorsius, sed omnēs tamen advorsīs volneribus conciderant. Catilīna vērō longē ā suīs inter hostium cadāvera repertus est, paululum etiam spīrāns ferōciamque animī, quam habuerat vīvos, in voltū retinēns.

1. **What gave the veterans encouragement?** (421)
2. **What does Catiline do for men he sees experiencing difficulty?** (422–423)
3. **Find evidence to support Sallust's evaluation of Catiline's efforts.** (424–425)
4. **What must have been Petreius' opinion of Catiline's courage before the battle?** (426)
5. **In what sense does Catiline's death befit his social station as a patrician nobleman and his *prīstina dignitās*?** (430–432)
6. **How does Sallust give a touch of humanity to Catiline at his death?** (437–439)

Bronze cornū *found at Pompeii*

67

441 **ingenuus, -a, -um**, of free birth. Here the idea contrasts with **captus est**; in dying the rebels carried out Catiline's bidding (in his speech before the battle) that they not be captured and so lose their freedom. **suae hostiumque vītae**: standard idiom in which the possessive adjective takes the place of a pronoun in the genitive, "their own and their enemies' lives." **Vītae** is dative with **pepercerant**. **iuxtā**, equally, (here) not at all. The remark is ironical.

442 **Neque ... laetam aut incruentam**: the litotes draws attention to these details. **incruentus, -a, -um**, bloodless.

443 **strēnuissumus quisque**: "all the bravest men."

444 **vīsundī aut spoliandī grātiā**: **grātiā** + gerunds in the genitive expresses purpose. **vīsō, vīsere** (3), **vīsī, vīsum**, to go to see, visit.

445 **aliī, pars**: = **aliī, aliī**. Notice the heightened pathos of the chiasmus.

446 **hospes, hospitis** (m), guest, host. **cognātus, -ī** (m), kinsman, relation. The order **amīcum** (445) ... **hospitem** ... **cognātum** ascends in the nearness of the bond to the observer. **quī ... cognōscerent** (447): relative clause of characteristic.

447 **laetitia, -ae** (f), happiness, joy. **maeror, maerōris** (m), sorrow. **laetitia, maeror, lūctus atque gaudia**: the chiasmus poignantly intermingles the conflicting emotions felt by the survivors (note the adverb **variē**) and provides a neat "packaging" effect that draws Sallust's account to a tidy conclusion that may seem too abrupt for our expectations.

448 **agitābantur**: a striking *personification*, "continued to dart back and forth."

Sallust is at pains to depict, at the end, a Catiline that is a union of all qualities that marked this tragic man: determination, courage, and leadership, counterbalanced by murderousness and an insatiable drive to use others to further his own ambitions. The critical reader will want to keep in mind also Sallust's skill as a writer.: how he draws highly delineated contrasts between the stereotypes of political uprightness of the dim past and of selfishness and depravity in his own day. Consider as well Cicero's concerns: for his own skin, for the polish of his reputation as the establisher of his vaunted "harmony of the classes," for his goal, perhaps, to rival at home the storied achievements of Pompey the Great in the East in preserving Rome's empire, built at great cost to Romans. Depraved, criminal, and desperate anarchist Catiline may have been; he is also the perfect subject for Sallust's moralizing pen. It is necessary in reading this story to note carefully all sides of both the subject and the authors, and not to be seduced by any veil of romantic pathos Sallust may appear to draw over the end of the tale.

Great also was the self-sacrifice of the common soldiers. Mixed with their elation at winning, the loyalist army experienced profound grief at the destruction of fellow citizens.

440 Postrēmō ex omnī cōpiā neque in proeliō neque in fugā quisquam cīvis ingenuus captus est: ita cūnctī suae hostiumque vītae iuxtā pepercerant. Neque tamen exercitus populī Rōmānī laetam aut incruentam victōriam adeptus erat; nam strēnuissimus quisque aut occiderat in proeliō aut graviter volnerātus discesserat. Multī autem, quī ē castrīs vīsundī aut
445 spoliandī grātiā prōcesserant, volventēs hostīlia cadāvera, amīcum aliī, pars hospitem aut cognātum reperiēbant; fuēre item quī inimīcōs suōs cognōscerent. Ita variē per omnem exercitum laetitia, maeror, lūctus atque gaudia agitābantur.

1. **How many of Catiline's army of 3,000 men were captured?** (440–441)
2. **Explain the irony behind the clause, *ita cūnctī ... pepercerant.*** (441)
3. **What distinguished the bravest of Petreius' Romans?** (443–444)
4. **What was found by those who visited the battlefield afterwards?** (444–447)
5. **Sallust seems to want to leave us with doubts: pathos mingles with horror, tragedy with triumph. How does he achieve this blended effect? Explain his motive.**

Excerpts have been taken from the works listed below and have been grouped
under three broad headings.

Hardy, E.G. *The Catilinarian Conspiracy in Its Context: A Re-Study of the
Evidence.* Oxford: Blackwell, 1924. Reprinted, New York: Ams Press, 1976.
Hutchinson, Lester. *The Conspiracy of Catiline.* New York: Barnes & Noble,
1967.
Mommsen, Theodor. *The History of Rome.* Rev. Trans. of 1868 by W.P. Dick-
son. Vol. 4. London: J.M. Dent, Everyman's Library, n. d.
Seager, R. "Iusta Catilinae," *Historia* 22 (1973): 240–248.

THE SUBORDINATE PLAYERS

To what extent is the failure of the conspiracy attributable to the incompetence of Catiline's lieutenants? In the first of the excerpts printed below,
Robin Seager argues that Manlius and Catiline were not necessarily in league
to sponsor an armed revolution. In the second excerpt, Seager explores the
possibility that Catiline himself may have been driven to espouse the cause
of Manlius and his band of desperadoes as a last resort against the incrimina-
tions of his political enemy Cicero. In the third excerpt, by contrast, Lester
Hutchinson adopts the more conventional view that Catiline was the ringleader of a concerted effort to overthrow the government, and attributes the
failure of the plot to the incompetence of Catiline's lieutenants in Rome.

a. Seager, pp. 240–241

Catilina and Manlius

For Cicero Manlius is throughout a tool of Catilina and his rising a part
of Catilina's master plan. . . . That Manlius was linked with Catilina
cannot be disputed; the nature of their association is quite clear. At the
elections of 63 Catilina was supported by a large band of discontented
Sullan colonists from Arretium and Faesulae, with a sprinkling of those
who had lost their land to make way for the veterans, and Manlius was
the leader of these men. . . . In the light of this close and public connection it was easy for Cicero to maintain that Manlius' rising had been
planned in advance by Catilina. But there are strong grounds for rejecting
this assertion.

    In the first place Manlius took up arms too early, on 27 October (Sall.
Cat. 30.1, cf. Cic. *Cat.* 1.7). Yet the other conspirators, according to
Cicero, were not even assigned their duties until the meeting in the

house of Laeca on the night of 5 or 6 November. If the senate had seen fit to exert itself, Manlius could have been, if not crushed, at least cut off from Rome, almost before that meeting was alleged to have taken place. So if Manlius rose as part of a prearranged plan, the date chosen for his rising is odd to say the least. But the key factor is his offer to Marcius Rex (Sall. *Cat.* 33). The precise degree of Sallust's accuracy is hardly relevant here; if Manlius sent any message *huiusce modi*, he cannot have been part of a project for total revolution. In brief he volunteered to surrender if the grievances of his followers were redressed. It is surely incredible that the second-in-command of a carefully organised military coup would offer to lay down his arms before his commander had even taken the field. But if Manlius was the independent leader of a peasant's revolt, then everything falls into place. He and his supporters had backed Catilina at the elections in the hope that as consul he would try to improve their situation. His failure destroyed their last chance of legal redress, and so in desperation they rebelled. But they were at pains to make it clear why they had taken this course, and it is plain that, if the senate had shown any sincere inclination to right their wrongs, Manlius would have been happy to surrender at once, regardless of any supposed designs of Catilina's.

The only evidence connecting Catilina with Manlius' rebellion before he actually joined it is the story that Catilina sent to Manlius a legionary standard that had long been kept in his house (Cic. *Cat.* 1.24, cf. 2.13). This standard was undoubtedly in Catilina's possession at the battle of Pistoria (Sall. *Cat.* 59.3). But when it left Catilina's house is another matter: neither Cicero nor anybody else would have been able to check the veracity of his claim that the eagle had already gone ahead at the time when Catilina himself left the city. In a matter where Cicero knew that he could lie with impunity it is surely better to reject his statement in favour of Sallust's evidence for Manlius' independence.

b. Seager, pp. 247–248

Catilina's Actions

The first question that must be asked is why did Catilina leave Rome when he did. If he hoped for revolution but was innocent of any plot, the wisest course would surely have been to sit it out, steeling himself to bear Cicero's provocations, in the hope that Pompeius' return would provide opportunities. The answer no doubt lies in Catilina's character and in the developing situation. The *First Catilinarian* marked an intensification of Cicero's hostility towards him, while the rising of Manlius pointed to a possible way out. Before, Cicero might have been endured, and anyway there was nowhere to go. Now Catilina's pride could bear no more and Manlius offered an escape, however desperate.

But although the possibility of joining Manlius may have contributed to Catilina's decision to leave Rome, it is far from certain that he had made up his mind to rebel before he left. In the *First Catilinarian* Cicero repeatedly asserts that Catilina is going to leave the city for Manlius' camp and urges him to do so without delay (Cic. *Cat.* 1.9f., 12f., 18, 24, 30, 33). Yet even here he faces the possibility that instead Catilina will go into exile (Cic. *Cat.* 1.20, 23). After Catilina's departure his friends maintained that, unable to endure any longer the incessant persecution to which Cicero had subjected him, he was indeed going into exile at Massilia (Cic. *Cat.* 2.12 ff.). Beneath the scorn that Cicero heaps on this suggestion it is easy to detect a nagging uncertainty—he believed that Catilina would go to Manlius, but he was not absolutely sure.

On his journey Catilina sent a number of letters claiming that he had been falsely accused, but that since he was unable to resist his *inimici* he would yield to fortune and go into exile at Massilia (Sall. *Cat.* 34.2). It is tempting to accept this claim at its face value, simply because if it was false it was utterly pointless. Catilina stood to gain nothing by telling a lie that he knew would be exposed within a few days by his actions, and the same is true of his friends in Rome: unless they sincerely believed he was going into exile, they had no reason whatever to say so.

But the matter is not quite as simple as that, since Catilina took with him when he left his legionary standard and perhaps also *fasces* and other emblems of office. This proves that he at least envisaged the possibility of rebellion. It therefore seems likely that at the time he left Rome he had not yet finally made up his mind what to do, though the letters suggest that at the moment when they were written exile was uppermost in his thoughts. His letter to Catulus is consistent with this impression (Sall. *Cat.* 35). It was written before his departure from the city (Sall. *Cat.* 35.5). He will not, he says, offer a defence *in novo consilio*, but an explanation of his conduct. This explanation has nothing to do either with going into exile or with joining Manlius; it merely presents Catilina's views on the results of the consular elections of 64 and tells why he put forward a programme of reform at the elections of 63. Then he goes on: *hoc nomine satis honestas pro meo casu spes reliquae dignitatis conservandae sum secutus.* What did he mean by *novum consilium*, what were the *satis honestae spes*? In the letter there is no clear answer, and the words themselves could apply equally well to rebellion or retirement in the face of tyranny. Perhaps the wording reflects Catilina's own uncertainty; he may even deliberately have chosen ambiguous terms that would still hold good whatever his eventual decision.

It was probably only at Arretium that Catilina at last made up his mind (cf. Sall. *Cat.* 36.1). The senate too had not been sure; it was only when he committed himself that he and Manlius were declared *hostes* (Sall. *Cat.* 36.2). His choice needs little explanation. His *dignitas* had been intolerably impaired (cf. Sall. *Cat.* 35.3f.), and meditation on how best to preserve the remnants of it must have convinced him that rebellion, however hopeless, was a more honourable way out than exile. *Cum summa turpitudine in exilio aetatem agere*—so Sallust makes his Catilina describe the alternative he ultimately rejected (Sall. *Cat.* 58.13). Cicero too understood what drove Catilina; he had sensed that Catilina would, as he put it, prefer to die a brigand than live an exile (Cic. *Cat.* 2.16: *latrocinantem se interfici mallet quam exsulem vivere*). Such was the course that Catilina followed to the last, *memor generis atque pristinae suae dignitatis* (Sall. *Cat.* 60.7).

c. Hutchinson, pp. 161–162

Cicero had been right. As he predicted the fate of the conspiracy was decided in Rome. In fact it had been decided the moment Catiline had left the city, entrusting the execution of his plans to his divided and inefficient lieutenants. 'Had I not driven this man (Catiline), who is so active, so prepared, so cunning, so vigilant in evil, so industrious in crime, from his plots within the city to the open warfare of the field . . . I should not easily have removed from your necks so great a weight of evil. He would not have determined on the Saturnalia to massacre you; he would not have announced the destruction of the Republic, and even the very date of its ruin so long beforehand' (Cic. *Cat.* 3.17). Cicero's reluctant admiration for Catiline's qualities is measured by his contempt for his associates who allowed themselves to be trapped and taken like clumsy housebreakers. 'It is obvious that he was not with them; he would not have let the favourable opportunity pass; he was too clever to allow himself to be caught.' Catiline's fatal error then was in leaving Rome. He was not driven from the city, as Cicero boasted; he had decided to join the army in Etruria before he was denounced; at most Cicero by his attack had accelerated his departure. It was part of the general plan that Catiline should take command of Manlius' army, march with it on Rome, which in the hands of the insurgents, would be open to him. His error lay therefore not so much in leaving Rome as in being over-confident in the ability and resolution of his lieutenants, whom before leaving he had carefully instructed in the part they were to play in the concerted plan. Cethegus alone was loyal to these orders, opposing vigorously all proposals to delay the rising, but he was overruled by Lentulus, whose insubordination was matched only by his indecision.

THE INVOLVEMENT OF CAESAR AND CRASSUS

To what extent were the interests of Caesar and Crassus affected by the failure of Catiline's conspiracy? In the first of the excerpts below, Theodor Mommsen argues that Caesar and Crassus were undoubtedly supporters of Catiline and that they were placed in a difficult position by their ties to the plot once it had been exposed. Hardy, however, in the second excerpt stresses that the damage to these two powerful figures was minimal and that Caesar, in fact, emerged from the crisis with greater popularity among the common people than before.

d. Mommsen, pp. 170–171

The anarchist plot had thus been suppressed in the capital and in Italy with bloody violence; people were reminded of it merely by the criminal processes which in the Etruscan country towns and in the capital thinned the ranks of those affiliated to the beaten party, and by the large accessions to the robber bands of Italy—one of which, for instance, formed out of the remains of the armies of Spartacus and Catilina, was destroyed by a military force in 60 B.C. in the territory of Thurii. But it is important to keep in view that the blow fell by no means merely on the anarchists proper, who had conspired to set the capital on fire and had fought at Pistoria, but on the whole democratic party. That this party, and in particular Crassus and Caesar, had a hand in the game on the present occasion as well as in the plot of 66, may be regarded—not in a juristic, but in an historical, point of view—as an ascertained fact. The circumstance, indeed, that Catulus and the other heads of the senatorial party accused the leader of the democrats of complicity in the anarchist plot, and that the latter as senator spoke and voted against the brutal judicial murder contemplated by the oligarchy, could only be urged by partisan sophistry as any valid proof of his participation in the plans of Catilina. But a series of other facts is of more weight. According to express and irrefragable testimonies it was especially Crassus and Caesar that supported the candidature of Catilina for the consulship. When Caesar in 64 brought the executioners of Sulla before the commission for murder he allowed the rest to be condemned, but the most guilty and infamous of all, Catilina, to be acquitted. In the revelations of the 3rd of December, it is true, Cicero did not include among the names of the conspirators of whom he had information those of the two influential men; but it is notorious that the informers denounced not merely those against whom subsequently investigation was directed, but "many innocent" persons besides, whom the consul Cicero thought proper to erase from the list; and in later years, when he had no reason to disguise the truth, he expressly named Caesar among the accomplices. An indirect but very intelligible inculpation is implied also in the circumstance, that of the four persons arrested on the 3rd of December the two least dangerous, Statilius and Gabinius, were handed over to be guarded by the senators Caesar and Crassus; it was manifestly intended that these should either, if they allowed them to escape, be compromised in the view of public opinion as accessories, or, if they really detained them, be compromised in the view of their fellow-conspirators as renegades.

e. Hardy, pp. 102–104

But during the last weeks of December people in Rome troubled themselves little about Catiline's fate. The whole conspiracy had flickered out with the public exposure and arrest on the 3rd, and after the striking events of the 5th, Cicero was perhaps for the moment the hero of the hour. But the very suddenness of the collapse must have made the public soon realise that the whole affair had been unduly magnified, and probably Dio's judgment represents the more sober views of the time: (37.42.1 "The name of Catiline occupied a greater place in history than was deserved by the importance of his deeds thanks to the renown of Cicero and the speeches of Cicero against him.")

Undoubtedly Cicero had increased Catiline's reputation. Once put upon the right track by Crassus, and aided by some good fortune, he had taken adequate precautions, and carried the affair through with steadiness and judgment. He had no doubt persuaded himself that the state was in real and imminent danger, and he had accepted what he knew to be considerable personal risk (*mei capitis periculi*) in his final act. He was almost certainly suspicious of the part played by Crassus and Caesar in spite of warnings received by them, but he was painfully conscious that they were not materially affected by the collapse of the conspiracy. He probably regretted Cato's innuendos in the senate, and he must have been embarrassed by the behaviour of the extreme *optimates* as well as some of the *equites*.

According to authorities used by Plutarch (*Caes.* 7) the latter needed only a sign from Cicero to attack Caesar as he left the senate after the debate on the 5th. The story may be true, notwithstanding Cicero's silence as to the incident in his history of his consulship. Still more awkward were the disclosures of Vettius, almost certainly prompted by men like Catulus and Piso. Dio (37.41) gives a vague account of the reckless charges brought by this informer, but Suetonius (*Iul.* 17) declares that he made special charges against Caesar, offering to produce a letter written by him to Catiline. As Curius made similar charges in the senate, Caesar thought it worthwhile publicly to call upon Cicero to say whether he had or had not received from him certain information concerning the conspiracy. Cicero acknowledged that this was the case, and Vettius and Curius were discredited. The incident was the occasion for a popular demonstration, which proved that Caesar's reserved attitude during the crisis had increased rather than diminished his influence with the populace. According to Plutarch the crowd, knowing what was afoot, waited outside the senate till Caesar appeared in safety, while, if Suetonius is to be believed, Vettius narrowly escaped being torn in pieces in the forum.

THE PROBLEMS LEFT UNRESOLVED

To what extent was the victory over Catiline and the conspirators merely temporary? The first excerpt below from Mommsen takes up the narrative of events after the arrest of Catiline's associates in December and examines the legality and expediency of the Senate's decision to execute the conspirators who had been taken into custody. In the second excerpt, Hutchinson touches upon the same issue and points up as well some of the other factors that were soon to endanger Cicero personally and weaken the ascendancy of the Senate.

f. Mommsen, pp. 167–169

In a tolerably well-ordered commonwealth the matter would now have been politically at an end, and the military and the tribunals would have undertaken the rest. But in Rome matters had come to such a pitch, that the government was not even in a position to keep a couple of noblemen of note in safe custody. The slaves and freedmen of Lentulus and of the others arrested were stirring; plans, it was alleged, were contrived to liberate them by force from the private houses in which they were detained; there was no lack—thanks to the anarchist doings of recent years—of ringleaders in Rome who contracted at a certain rate for riots and deeds of violence; Catilina, in fine, was informed of what had occurred, and was near enough to attempt a *coup de main* with his bands. How much of these rumours was true, we cannot tell; but there was ground for apprehension, because, agreeably to the constitution, neither troops nor even a respectable police force were at the command of the government in the capital, and it was in reality left at the mercy of every gang of banditti. The idea was suggested of precluding all possible attempts at liberation by the immediate execution of the prisoners. Constitutionally, this was not possible. According to the ancient and sacred right of appeal, a sentence of death could only be pronounced against the Roman burgess by the whole body of burgesses, and not by any other authority; and, as the courts formed by the body of burgesses had themselves become antiquated, a capital sentence was no longer pronounced at all. Cicero would gladly have rejected the hazardous suggestion; indifferent as in itself the legal question might be to the advocate, he knew well how very useful it is to an advocate to be called liberal, and he showed little desire to separate himself for ever from the democratic party by shedding this blood. But those around him, and particularly his aristocratic wife, urged him to crown his services to his country by this bold step; the consul like all cowards anxiously endeavouring to avoid the appearance of cowardice, and yet trembling before the formidable responsibility, in his distress convoked the senate, and left it to that body to decide as to life or death of the four prisoners. This indeed had no meaning; for as the senate was constitutionally even less entitled to act than the consul, all the responsibility still devolved rightfully on the latter; but when was cowardice ever consistent? Caesar made every exertion to save the prisoners, and his speech, full of covert threats as to the future inevitable vengeance of the democracy, made the deepest impression. Although all the consulars and the great majority of the senate had already declared for the execution, most of them, with Cicero at their head, seemed now once more inclined to keep within the limits of the law. But when Cato in pettifogging fashion brought the champions of the milder view into suspicion of being accomplices of the plot, and pointed to the preparation for liberating the prisoners by a street-riot, he succeeded in throwing the waverers into a fresh alarm, and in securing a majority for the immediate executions of the transgressors.

The execution of the decree naturally devolved on the consul, who had called it forth. Late on the evening of the 5th of December the prisoners were brought from their previous quarters, and conducted across the market-place still densely crowded by men to the prison in which criminals condemned to death were wont to be kept. It was a subterranean vault, twelve feet deep, at the foot of the Capitol, which formerly had served as a well-house. The consul himself conducted Lentulus, and praetors the others, all attended by strong guards; but the attempt at rescue, which had been expected, did not take place. No one knew whether the prisoners were being conveyed to a secure place of custody or to the scene of execution. At the door of the prison they were handed over to the triumvirs who conducted the executions, and were strangled in the subterranean vault by torchlight. The consul had waited before the door till the executions were accomplished, and then with his loud well-known voice proclaimed over the Forum to the multitude waiting in silence, "They are dead." Till far on in the night the crowds moved through the streets and exultingly saluted the consul, to whom they believed that they owed the security of their houses and their property. The senate ordered public festivals of gratitude and the first men of the nobility, Marcus Cato and Quintus Catulus, saluted the author of the sentence of death with the name—now heard for the first time—of a "father of his fatherland."

But it was a dreadful deed, and all the more dreadful that it appeared to a whole people great and commendable. Never perhaps has a commonwealth more lamentably declared itself bankrupt than did Rome through this resolution—adopted in cold blood by the majority of the government and approved by public opinion—to put to death in all haste a few political prisoners, who were no doubt culpable according to the laws, but had not forfeited life; because, forsooth, the security of the prisons was not to be trusted, and there was no sufficient police. It was the humorous trait seldom wanting to an historical tragedy that this act of the most brutal tyranny had to be carried out by the most unstable and timid of all Roman statesmen, and that the "first democratic consul" was selected to destroy the palladium of the ancient freedom of the Roman commonwealth, the right of *provocatio*.

The optimates rejoiced. Catiline was dead, his soldiers slaughtered. The fearful fate of Lentulus and his associates should deter others from following the path of rebellion. The surviving conspirators of high rank, including Porcius Laeca, C. Cornelius, L. Vargunteius, Servius Sulla and P. Autronius, were prosecuted and driven into exile. Rome was safe again for the best people.

All this they owed to the skill and resolution of the retiring consul, Cicero. They showered compliments upon him and their praise was only exceeded by that which he bestowed upon himself.

But while they enjoyed their victory they neglected to inquire into the causes of the rebellion. They could not see that the Republic in which they alone prospered was mortally sick. They were blind to the dangers that arose from debt-ridden citizens, expropriated farmers, three hundred and twenty thousand unemployed loafers dependent on the dole, sullen slaves and resentful freedmen. They could feel the wind of new concepts sweeping in from more advanced civilisations and acting as a catalyst on old discontents. And while they enthused over the defeat of Catiline, they failed to observe Caesar, who coldly, systematically and ruthlessly had resumed his march towards the sovereign power.

They saw danger only from Pompey, but it was a limited danger. Pompey was essentially conservative, and had he made himself dictator, while a few heads would have rolled, he would have done nothing to damage the economic and social structure that created the dominant class. In fact he did nothing at all on his return, and when the optimates recovered from their astonishment they were stupid enough to antagonise him, thus driving him into the arms of Caesar.

If the optimates were uneasy at all it was at the prospect of a swing in public opinion towards the popular party, and the denunciation by some demagogue of their high-handed and illegal action in executing the five conspirators. In this event they had their scapegoat ready, decked in the sacrificial garments. Having done his job, Cicero was expendable. He was not one of them, but a conceited upstart. They were jealous of his success, resentful of the airs he assumed and bored by his constant and inopportune boasting. No doubt many applauded the jibe made by the younger Torquatus that Cicero was the third foreign king to have reigned in Rome after Numa and Tarquinius. In the same speech, Torquatus took pains to suggest to the crowd that Cicero alone was responsible for the death of Lentulus (Cic. *Sull*. 22; 29–33).

Cicero had, of course, foreseen that an attempt would be made to make him the scapegoat, and had appealed in his speeches against Catiline both for the protection of the people and the Senate. He was vain enough to believe that he had the affection of the people and the admiration of the Senate. When laying down his office as consul he was forbidden by the tribune Metellus to make the customary speech to the assembled people on the ground that a man who had put citizens to death unheard ought not to be permitted to speak for himself. Cicero, who was never at a loss on these occasions, thereupon shouted out that he had saved the Republic and the city from ruin, a statement that was confirmed by the crowd with the universal shout that what he had said was true. The incident merely encouraged him in the belief that the mob was on his side; he did not attend to the sinister implication behind the tribune's action.

EXERCISES

Lines 1–130

1. *Change each ablative singular to a plural and each plural to a singular.*
coniūrātiōne, perīculō, vultū, vīribus, rē, modīs, lūxuriā, discordiīs,
quō, hīs (*f*).

2. *Combine the two sentences in each pair by changing the first into an ablative absolute. Then translate each new sentence.*

a. Comitia habita sunt. Cōnsulēs dēclārātī sunt M. Tullius et C. Antōnius.

b. Maximum facinus incēpimus. Tandem lībertātem pulcherrimam habēbimus.

c. Arma in Etrūriā dēpōne. Antōnius tuīs mīlitibus parcet.

3. *Write the form of the adjective (given in parentheses) that correctly modifies each noun following it.*

(varius) fortūnā, vim, cupiditātī, diērum, sceleribus.

(audāx) scelus, adulēscentī, sapientiam, artium, exercitū.

4. *Translate:*

a. Nisi Pompeius in extrēmīs terrīs bellum gereret, Catilīna rēs novās
nōn temptāret.

b. Sī mihi satis crēdētis, rēs opportūna nōbīs cadet.

c. Fulvia sī Quīntum amāvisset, ad Cicerōnem cōnsilia Catilīnae nōn rettulisset.

d. Nisi Catilīna arma in urbe cēlāvisset, populus eī favēret.

e. Cūrius sī Cicerōnem dē perīculō praemonēre vult, nūntium per Fulviam
mittit.

5. *Transform the following statements into direct commands using the imperative or subjunctive as required. Then translate.*

a. Vōs omnēs estis semper intentī parātīque.

b. Antōnius nōn contrā rem pūblicam sentit.

c. Comitia ad cōnsulēs dēclārandōs habēmus.

d. Tū nōn arbitrāris nōs nihil scīre.

6. *Combine each pair of sentences by converting the second sentence into a relative clause dependent on the first. Then translate your new complex sentence.*

a. Catilīna cōnscientiam scelerum artibus auxerat. Eās artēs suprā memorāvī.

b. Omnēs vōs ea iam audīvistis. Ea mente agitāvī.

c. Ēn illa lībertās! Illam saepe optāvistis.

d. Cicerō effēcerat ut Q. Cūrius cōnsilia sibi prōderet. Dē Cūriō paulō ante
scrīpsī.

e. Catilīna rem pūblicam dēlēre cōnātus est. Reī pūblicae (*gen.*) salūtem omnēs
bonī dēfendere dēbēbant.

7. *Translate:*

Catiline, a Roman senator, whose mind always wished for too much, decided to
seize mastery over (**dominātiō** + *gen.*) the government. About the first of June,
after assembling some friends and dependents, he revealed to them a plan he

dared to set in motion (**capere**). "Let your hearts burn every day with a desire for freedom! Let's seize freedom for ourselves!" But the next year a woman named Fulvia eventually told Marcus Cicero, the consul, about the plot. After Catiline had sent Gaius Manlius to Faesulae to enlist an army, Cicero addressed the Senate: "For how long will Catiline abuse our patience? Senators, he plots revolution. Exact (**sūmō**) from (**dē**) him the punishment he deserves."

Lines 131–229

8. *Change each singular to a plural and each plural to a singular.*
   hostium, nōbīs (*dat.*), faciēī (*gen.*), metuī, mūrōrum, custōdī, hominis, calamitātibus (*dat.*), cōpiārum, praesidiō (*dat.*).

9. *Rewrite to introduce each subordinate clause with* **cum**, *changing the mood as required. Then translate the revised sentence.*
   a. Ubi advesperāscēbat, armātī cum magistrātibus ad pontem Mulvium pervēnērunt.
   b. Quod haec ita sunt, Catilīna, ēdūc tēcum omnīs tuōs ad Manliāna castra.
   c. Postquam cōnsul assēdit, Catilīna cum patribus dissimulandī causā agere coepit.

10. *Write one direct question for which the statement is the answer, and then translate both.*
    a. Iove urbem custōdiente, hanc tam īnfestam pestem effūgimus.
    b. Hāc nocte ad pontem Mulvium omnēs perveniēmus.
    c. Lēgātī Allobrogum Cicerōnem convēnērunt coniūrātiōnis patefaciendae causā.

11. *Combine each pair of simple sentences by converting the first sentence into a participial phrase. Then translate the new sentence.*
    a. Īnsidiae prope Tiberim flūmen collocātae sunt. Īnsidiae extrā urbem sunt.
    b. Catilīna ab inimīcīs circumventus est. Catilīna praeceps agitur.
    c. Litterae lēgātīs Allobrogum ad suōs cīvīs redientibus mandātae sunt. Litterae ad Catilīnam mittēbantur.

12. *Translate:*
    a. Cōnsul omnibus virīs fortibus ostendit quid fierī placēret.
    b. Allobrogēs nōn intellegunt utrum Cicerō sibi crēdat necne.
    c. Catilīna mīrātus erat quānam dē causā litterae integrīs signīs praetōribus trāditae essent.

13. *From each direct command write an indirect command dependent upon the main clause given in parentheses. Translate the new sentence.*
    a. "Impetum in Volturcium facite." (Praetor adulēscentīs ex praefectūrā Reātīnā dēlēctōs hortābātur . . .)
    b. "Opēs factiōnis cōnfirmāte." (Catilīna, antequam ad castra profectus est, Lentulō cēterīsque mandāverat . . .)
    c. "Nōlī Lentulō cōnfīdere." (Lēgātī Allobrogum cōnsulem rogant . . .)

14. *Translate:*
    Daily the number of disloyal citizens increased who were flocking to Manlius' camp to join Catiline's army. The consul wondered why he had not killed Catiline earlier in order to protect his country from this grief. Then Catiline himself left Rome to join Manlius. Finally, as it happened, some ambassadors of the Allobroges, a Gallic people living beyond the Alps, came to the consul. They brought with them letters, signed by some senators in Rome; these senators had asked them to take the letters to Manlius in Etruria. Cicero set an ambush at the Mulvian Bridge, seized the ambassadors and the unopened (*use ablative absolute*, "their seals intact") letters, and brought them to the Senate in Rome. Cicero was glad that he could disclose the conspiracy (*use an indirect statement*) and that the senators would finally believe him.

15. *Fill in the blanks to match the English cues. Translate the entire sentence.*
Lēgātī Allobrogum, quī _____ (to the Senate in Rome) vēnērunt,

_____ (at the homes of several senators) _____
(in Rome) manēre mālunt; sed, cum _____ (from Rome)
discesserint, _____ (to their own people) iterum statim
properāre valdē volent.

16. *Connect each pair of sentences into a single complex sentence by converting each direct quotation into an indirect statement governed by the verb in the first sentence; make all appropriate changes. Then translate.*

　a. Frequēns senātus paulō ante iūdicāvit. "Eī hominēs contrā rem pūblicam fēcērunt."

　b. Sīlānus cēnset. "Coniūrātī poenās dare dēbent."

　c. Lentulus sermōnibus adfirmāre solitus erat. "Ego tertius sum cui librī Sibyllīnī rēgnum praedicāvērunt."

17. *Convert each question below into a statement followed by a purpose clause that answers the question. Base your purpose clause upon the clues found in the text as indicated by the line numbers in parentheses. Pay attention to the sequence of tenses. Translate your new sentences.*

　a. Cūr Decimus Sīlānus dīxit quae dīxerat? (268–269)

　b. Cūr cōnsul virīs armātīs senātum circumdedit? (275)

　c. Cūr in aliōs parricīdās patrēs quid statuerent cōnsīderāre dēbuērunt? (289)

18. *Fill in the blanks with perfect participles of the verbs in parentheses. Use correct agreement of gender, case, and number. Then translate.*

　a. Senātus Volturciō quid accidisset _____ lībenter pepercit. (fatērī)

　b. Senātōrem, ex Gabiniō audīre _____ multōs in eā coniūrātiōne esse, dē itinere interrogāvērunt. (solēre)

　c. Itaque Cicerō praesidia addet, Lentulō et Cethēgō (*abl.*) lībertōs suōs in audāciam ōrāre _____ . (cōnārī)

　d. Exempla mala, cōnsul, verēre ex rēbus bonīs _____ . (orīrī)

19. *Translate.*

　a. Patribus cōnscrīptīs persuādendī causā Caesar bene et compositē dē vītā et morte disseruit.

　b. Catilīna dissimulandī causā aut suī expurgandī in senātum incessit.

　c. Caesar in senātum ad Cicerōnī resistendum properāverat.

20. *Translate.*

Volturcius, who had revealed to the Senate all that he knew, was rewarded. The letters of the conspirators (**coniūrātī, -ōrum**) to Catiline near Faesulae were produced and read; moreover, the Allobrogian emissaries were thanked because they had been a help to the Romans. Even though some of the arrested conspirators tried to escape, the consul, seizing his opportunity, convened the Senate to ask what should be done (*use* **agere**) to them (*use* **dē** + *abl.*). Although various men urged various solutions, Cicero promised to do the Senate's bidding, asking only that, if the conspirators should win out, the Senate would remember and protect his son.

Lines 339–448

21. *Turn the second sentence of each pair into a result clause. In the main clause use the word in parentheses. Translate the new complex sentence you have composed.*

a. Catō disertē loquitur. (tam) Facile senātōribus persuādēbit.

b. Catilīna magna scelera ausus est. (tantus) Senātus eum patriae hostem iūdicāvit.

c. Multī armātī ā cōpiīs dīlāpsī sunt. (tot) Catilīna satis mīlitum nōn habet ad Metellī exercitum superandum.

22. *Fill in the blanks by translating into Latin the English in parentheses.*

a. Sociīs Rōmae comprehēnsīs et cōpiīs haud bene armātīs,

_____ ? (what is

Catiline to do?)

b. _____ cōnsul prius Catilīnam _____ quam

ad pugnam itum est! (If only . . . had arrested)

c. _____ perfugae Rōmam sēditiōnis faciendae causā

_____ ! (Let not . . . return)

23. *Complete by choosing the correct alternative, and then translate the sentence.*

a. Cōnsulātum adipīscī Catilīna _____ iam cōnātur. (duōs annōs/duōbus annīs)

b. Lentulus et cēterī coniūrātī exitium vītae in Tulliānō

_____ invēnērunt. (Nōnīs Decembribus/a. d. iii Nōnās Decembrēs)

24. *Change each sentence into a clause of fearing governed by one of these expressions:* **timor est/erat, timeō/timuī, vereor/veritus sum,** *or* **perīculum est/fuit.**

a. Senātōrēs dē coniugibus ac līberīs, dē ārīs ac focīs dīligenter nōn dēcernent.

b. Senātus in Catōnis sententiam discessit.

25. *Convert each clause in the left-hand column to a* **cum** *clause governed by the most suitable main clause on the right. Change the mood of underlined verbs as required.*

a. Caesar misericordiam prōpōnit,

b. Cicerō Lentulum et cēterōs coniūrātōs ante comitia dūcere dēbuit,

c. Catilīna suīs labōrantibus succurrēbat, omnia prōvidēbat, et multum ipse pugnābat,

i. in carcerem ad gulās frangendās statim mīsit.

ii. nē ūnus quidem cīvis ingenuus ex cōpiīs Catilīnae superfuit vel vīvus captus est.

iii. patrēs, familiārum et urbis memorēs, Catōnis sententiam probāvērunt.

26. *Translate.*

Cato urged the senators to fear for their lives, their families, their homes, and the Roman state; for [he said that] he wondered if they realized that that army was intending to act as the friends of Catiline had decreed.

Sallust tells us that a large number of Catiline's forces in Etruria began to slip away; that he realized that his army was shut off by the mountains and his enemies' forces; and that, when the battle was finished, everyone marveled at how great had been the determination (use **vīs animī**) in Catiline's army.

Thus a force of unarmed highway robbers, of whom some hoped for a fresh start economically (use **novae tabulae,** *f pl*), others wanted to lessen (use **minuere**) the Senate's power, for the sake of greater liberty dared to resist two armies sent against them by the state. How are we to think of them (use **exīstimāre**)?

VOCABULARY

A

ab, **ā** (+ *abl.*), from, away from, by

*__absum__, **abesse** (*irreg.*), **āfuī**, to be away, absent, missing

ac = **atque**

accēdō, **-ere** (3), **-ssī**, **-ssum**, to approach, go toward

*__accendō__, **-dere** (3), **-dī**, **-sum**, to set on fire, inflame

accidō, **-ere** (3), **-ī**, to happen

accipiō, **-ipere** (3), **-ēpī**, **-eptum**, to receive, accept

ācer, **ācris**, **ācre**, sharp, keen, eager

*__acerbus__, **-a**, **-um**, bitter, rough, coarse, violent

aciēs, **-ēī** (*f*), line of battle

ad (+ *acc.*), to, toward, near, at

*__addō__, **-ere** (3), **-idī**, **-itum**, to add

*__addūcō__, **-cere** (3), **-xī**, **-ctum**, to bring

adgredior, **-dī** (3), **-ssus sum**, to attack

adhūc, so far, up until now

*__adipīscor__, **-ipīscī** (3), **-eptus sum**, to obtain, get

*__adiungō__, **-gere** (3), **-xī**, **-ctum**, to join up with

*__adpetēns__, **-ntis** (+ *gen.*), covetous (of), greedy (for)

adsum, **-esse** (*irreg.*), **-fuī**, to be present

adulēscēns, **-ntis** (*m*), young man

adversus, **-a**, **-um**, opposite

aequus, **-a**, **-um**, level, favorable, equal

aes, **aeris** (*n*), copper, bronze

*__aes aliēnum__, **aeris aliēnī** (*n*), debt, indebtedness

aetās, **-ātis** (*f*), age, time of life

aeternus, **-a**, **-um**, everlasting, eternal, endless

ager, **agrī** (*m*), field, territory

*__agitō__ (1), to hunt, pursue (a course of action, rouse

agō, **agere** (3), **ēgī**, **āctum**, to do, act, drive

aliēnus, **-a**, **-um**, foreign, another's, unfavorable

aliquī, **aliqua**, **aliquod**, some, any

aliter, otherwise

alius, **-a**, **-ud**, other, another

*__Allobrogēs__, **-um** (*m pl*), (tribe of) the Allobroges (in Gaul)

alter, **-era**, **-erum**, the other, the second

alter . . . alter, the one . . . the other

altus, **-a**, **-um**, high, deep

amīcitia, **-ae** (*f*), friendship

amīcus, **-ī** (*m*), friend

āmittō, **-ittere** (3), **-īsī**, **-issum**, to lose

amō (1), to love

amplius, more, more than

amplus, **-a**, **-um**, large, spacious, distinguished

an, or, whether

anima, **-ae** (*f*), breath, soul, life

animadvertō, **-tere** (3), **-tī**, **-sum**, to notice

animus, **-ī** (*m*), mind, courage

annus, **-ī** (*m*), year

ante (+ *acc.*), before

anteā, previously

*__antecapiō__, **-capere** (3), **-cēpī**, **-ceptum**, to take action beforehand

antīquus, **-a**, **-um**, ancient, former

aperiō, **-īre** (4), **-uī**, **-tum**, to open

appellō (1), to name, call, address

apud (+ *acc.*), in the presence of, among, with, at the house of

āra, **-ae** (*f*), altar, (figuratively) home

arbitror (1), to think

arcessō, **-ere** (3), **-īvī**, **-ītum**, to summon, invite

arma, **-ōrum** (*n pl*), arms, weapons

armātus, **-ī** (*m*), armed man

armō (1), to arm

*__asper__, **-era**, **-erum**, rough, hard, adverse

at, but

atque, **ac**, and

auctor, **-ōris** (*m*), promoter, sponsor, authority

auctōritās, **-ātis** (*f*), authority, influence

*__audācia__, **-ae** (*f*), daring, boldness

audāx, **-ācis**, bold, daring

audeō, **-dēre** (2), **ausus sum**, to dare

audiō (4), to hear

augeō, **-gēre** (2), **-xī**, **-ctum**, to enlarge, increase

aut, or

aut . . . aut, either . . . or

autem, moreover, however

B

bellum, **-ī** (*n*), war

82

bene, well
beneficium, -ī (n), (act of) kindness, service
bonus, -a, -um, good
brevis, -is, -e, short

C

cadō, -ere (3), cecidī, cāsum, to fall, die
caedēs, -is (f), slaughter
calamitās, -ātis (f), disaster
campus, -ī (m), plain, field
capiō, -ere (3), cēpī, captum, to take, capture
*capitālis, -is, -e, capital, concerning one's life
carcer, -ris (m), prison
cārus, -a, -um, dear
castra, -ōrum (n pl), camp
cāsus, -ūs (m), chance, accident
causa, -ae (f), cause, reason
causā (with preceding gen.), for the sake of, for the purpose of
*caveō, -ēre (2), cāvī, cautum, to beware
cēdō, -dere (3), -ssī, -ssum, to go, give way, yield
*cēnseō, -ēre (2), -uī, -um, to be of the opinion
cernō, -ere (3), crēvī, crētum, to see, distinguish, discern
certō (1), to struggle, contend, vie
*certō, certainly, surely
certus, -a, -um, fixed, certain, sure
cēterī, -ae, -a (pl), the rest of, the other(s)
*cēterum (adv.), for the rest, however that may be, still
circiter, about, approximately
circum (+ acc.), around
circumdō, -are (1), -edī, -atum, to surround
*cīvīlis, -is, -e, of a citizen, civil
cīvis, -is (m/f), citizen
cīvitās, -ātis (f), state, citizenship
clārus, -a, -um, clear, bright, famous
claudō, -dere (3), -sī, -sum, to close
cliēns, -ntis (m), client, follower, dependent
coepī, coepisse (irreg.), coeptum, to have begun
cognōscō, -ōscere (3), -ōvī, -itum, to learn, (perfect) to know
cohors, -rtis (f), cohort
collēga, -ae (m), colleague
comes, -itis (m/f), companion
*comitātus, -ūs (m), escort, retinue, company
*comitia, -ōrum (n pl), assembly (of the people for voting), election
commendō (1), to entrust, commend
committō, -ittere (3), -mīsī, -missum, to commit, entrust, join (battle)
*commoror (1), to linger, tarry, stop
commūnis, -is, -e, common
comparō (1), to couple, match in pairs
comperiō, -īre (4), -ī, -tum, to discover, find out
complūrēs, -ēs, -a, several, many, a great many

*comprehendō, -dere (3), -dī, -sum, to seize, arrest
concēdō, -dere (3), -ssī, -ssum, to yield, concede, grant
*concitō (1), to stir up, urge on
condiciō, -ōnis (f), condition, terms
cōnfertus, -a, -um, thick, crowded together
cōnficiō, -icere (3), -ēcī, -ectum, to finish, accomplish
cōnfirmō (1), to strengthen, assert
*coniungō, -gere (3), -xī, -ctum, to join together, link
coniūnx, -ugis (m/f), spouse
*coniūrātiō, -ōnis (f), conspiracy, plot
coniūrō (1), to conspire, plot
conlocō (1), to place, station
cōnor (1), to try
*conparō = comparō
cōnscrībō, -bere (3), -psī, -ptum, to enlist, enroll
*cōnservō (1), to retain, preserve
*cōnsīderō (1), to contemplate
cōnsīdō, -sīdere (3), -sēdī, to encamp, sit down, settle down
cōnsilium, -ī (n), plan, counsel
cōnstituō, -uere (3), -uī, -ūtum, to set up, decide, determine
cōnsuētūdō, -inis (f), custom, habit
cōnsul, -is (m), consul (one of the two heads of state in Rome)
cōnsulāris, -is, -e, consular, of the consul, (noun) an ex-consul
*cōnsulātus, -ūs (m), consulship
cōnsulō, -ere (3), -uī, -tum, to consult, plan
*cōnsultō (1), to deliberate
contendō, -dere (3), -dī, -tum, to strive, hasten
contiō, -ōnis (f), assembly, address
contrā (+ acc.), against
*convincō, -incere (3), -īcī, -ictum, to convict, find guilty
*convocō (1), to call together, summon, assemble
cōpia, -ae (f), plenty, supply, (pl.) troops
corpus, -oris (n), body
cotīdiē, daily
crēdō, -ere (3), -idī, -itum, to believe, trust
cruciātus, -ūs (m), torture
crūdēlis, -is, -e, cruel
cruentus, -a, -um, bloody, bloodthirsty
cum (+ abl.), with
cum, when, since, although
cūnctī, -ae, -a, all
cupiō, -ere (3), -īvī, -ītum, to desire
cūra, -ae (f), care, concern
cūria, -ae (f), Senate House, the Senate, meeting of the Senate
*custōdia, -ae (f) custody
custōs, -ōdis (m), guard

D

dē (+ abl.), down from, about, concerning
dēcernō, -ernere (3), -rēvī, -rētum, to decide, decree

decet, -ēre (2), -uit (*impersonal*), it is fitting
*dēclārō (1), to announce, report
dēdūcō, -cere (3), -xī, -ctum, to lead down, draw off
dēfendō, -dere (3), -dī, -sum, to defend
deinde, next, then
dēleō, -ēre (2), -ēvī, -ētum, to destroy, wipe out
dēligō, -igere (3), -ēgī, -ēctum, to choose, select
dēmittō, -ittere (3), -īsī, -issum, to send down
*dēnique, at last, lastly, finally
dēprehendō, -dere (3), -dī, -sum, to seize, arrest
dēsīderō (1), to long for, miss, desire
*dēsignō (1), to mark out, pick out, choose in an election
   dēsignātus, -a, -um, elected
   cōnsul dēsignātus, the consul-elect
dēsum, -esse (*irreg.*), -fuī, to fail, be lacking
deus, -ī (*m*), god
dīcō, -cere (3), -xī, -ctum, to say, tell
diēs, -ēī (*m*), day
   *in diēs, daily
difficilis, -is, -e, difficult, hard
*dignitās, -ātis (*f*), prestige
dignus, -a, -um, worthy
dīligēns, -ntis, careful
*dīligentia, -ae (*f*), care, perseverance
*dīmittō, -ittere (3), -īsī, -issum, to dismiss, send away, let go
*discēdō, -dere (3), -ssī, -ssum, to go away, leave, depart
dīsiciō, -icere (3), -iēcī, -iectum, to scatter, rout
*dispōnō, -ōnere (3), -osuī, -ositum, to set out, arrange
disserō, -ere (3), -uī, -tum, to discuss, lecture on
*dissimulō (1), to disguise, conceal, pretend
diū, for a long time
*dīvitiae, -ārum (*f pl*), wealth, riches
dīvorsus, -a, -um, separated, different, diverse
dō, dare (1), dedī, datum, to give
doceō, -ēre (2), -uī, -tum, to teach, show
*dominātiō, -ōnis (*f*), tyranny, despotism
domus, -ūs (*f*), house, home
dubitō (1), to doubt, hesitate, be uncertain
dubius, -a, -um, doubtful, ambiguous
dūcō, -cere (3), -xī, -ctum, to lead, take, bring
dum, while, until
*dum (modo), provided that, if only
duo, duae, duo, two
dux, ducis (*m*), leader, general, commander

E

*ēdūcō, -cere (3), -xī, -ctum, to lead out or forth, draw
efficiō, -icere (3), -ēcī, -ectum, to cause, bring about

ego, nōs, I, we, us
*ēgredior, -edī (3), -essus sum, to go out, leave
ēgregius, -a, -um, extraordinary, excellent
enim, for
eō = ideō
eō, īre (*irreg.*), iī (īvī), itum, to go
*eō (*adv.*), to that place
eōdem, to the same place
equidem, indeed
equus, -ī (*m*), horse
*ēripiō, -ipere (3), -ipuī, -eptum, to rip out, tear away, snatch, deliver, rescue
et, and
   et . . . et, both . . . and
etiam, even, also
*ēveniō, -enīre (4), -ēnī, -entum, to come out, happen, occur
ex, ē (+ *abl.*), out of, from
exemplum, -ī, (*n*), example
exerceō (2), to train, exercise
exercitus, -ūs (*m*), army
exīstimō (= exīstumō) (1), to think
*exitium, -ī (*n*), destruction, ruin, death
expediō (4), to set free, make ready
experior, -īrī (4), -tus sum, to test, try out
explōrō (1), to reconnoiter, find out
expōnō, -ōnere (3), -osuī, -ositum, to explain, put forth, expose
exsilium, -ī (*n*), exile
exstinguō, -guere (3), -xī, -ctum, to destroy, extinguish
extrēmus, -a, -um, outermost, last

F

*faciēs, -ēī (*f*), face, features, appearance
facilis, -is, -e, easy
*facile, easily
*facinus, -oris (*n*), action, crime
faciō, -ere (3), fēcī, factum, to make, do
factiō, -ōnis (*f*), faction, party
facultās, -ātis (*f*), ability, possibility, chance
fallō, -lere (3), fefellī, -sum, to deceive, disappoint, prove false
familia, -ae (*f*), family, household, servants
familiāris, -is, -e, of the household, private
fānum, -ī (*n*), shrine
*fateor, -ērī (2), fassus sum, to confess, admit
fātum, -ī (*n*), fate, destiny
ferē, almost, usually
ferō, ferre (*irreg.*), tulī, lātum, to bring, carry, bear, endure
*ferōx, -ōcis, wild, savage, spirited, untamable, warlike
ferrum, -ī (*n*), iron, sword
*festīnō (1), to hasten, be active
fidēs, -eī (*f*), loyalty, faith, trust, credit
fīgō, -gere (3), -xī, -xum, to fix, fasten
fīlius, -ī (*m*), son
fingō, -ngere (3), -nxī, -ctum, to form, invent, pretend
fīnis, -is (*m*), limit, end (pl.) territory
fīō, fierī (*irreg.*), factus sum, to become, be

made, happen
firmus, -a, -um, strong, firm
*__focus, -ī__ (m), hearth, (figuratively) home
*__foedus, -a, -um,__ foul, hideous
forte, by chance
fortis, -is, -e, brave
fortūna, -ae (f), fortune, luck
frangō, -ngere (3), **frēgī, -ctum,** to break
frequēns, -entis, crowded, numerous
frōns, -ntis (f), front, forehead
fruor, -ī (3), **-ctus sum** (+ abl.), to enjoy
frustrā, in vain
fuga, -ae (f), escape, flight
fundō, -ere (3), **fūdī, fūsum,** to pour, rout
*__furor, -ōris__ (m), madness, frenzy

G

gaudium, -ī (n), joy
gēns, -tis (f), tribe, family, clan, nation
genus, -eris (n), kind, class, sort
gerō, -rere (3), **-ssī, -stum,** to carry, carry on, wage (war)
gladius, -ī (m), sword
glōria, -ae (f), fame, glory
grātia, -ae (f), favor, influence, (pl.) thanks
grātiā, for the sake of; (= **propter** + acc.) on account of
grātus, -a, -um, pleasing, welcome
gravis, -is, -e, heavy, severe, serious
grex, -egis (m), herd, flock

H

habeō (2), to have
*__haud,__ not, by no means
hic, haec, hoc, this, (pl.) these
homō, -inis (m), person, human being, man
honor (= **honōs**), **-ōris** (m), honor, office
*__horribilis, -is, -e,__ terrible, fearful, dreadful
hortor (1), to urge, encourage
hostis, -is (m), enemy

I

iam, already, by now
*__iam prīdem,__ long ago, well before now
ibi, there, in that place
īdem, eadem, idem, same
ideō, for that reason
idōneus, -a, -um, suitable
igitur, therefore
ignōrō (1), to be ignorant, not know
ille, illa, illud, that, the other (marking change of subject), (pl.) those
immortālis, -is, -e, immortal, undying, eternal
*__imperātor, -ōris__ (m), commander-in-chief
imperium, -ī (n), command, power
imperō (1), to command, order
impetus, -ūs (m), attack
*__imprīmīs,__ especially, particularly
improbus, -a, -um, wicked, depraved
in (+ abl.), in, on
in (+ acc.) into, onto, against
in prīmīs = imprīmīs

*__incendium, -ī__ (n), fire, blaze
incendō, -dere (3), **-dī, -sum,** to burn, set fire to
incipiō, -ipere (3), **-ēpī, -eptum,** to begin
incitō (1), to incite, arouse
*__indicium, -ī__ (n), disclosure, information, notice, charge
inermis, -is, -e, unarmed
īnferī, -ōrum (m pl), the dead (= those below), the lower world
*__īnfestus, -a, -um,__ hostile
*__ingenium, -ī__ (n), genius, talent, character, spirit
ingēns, -ntis, huge, very great, enormous
inimīcus, -a, -um, unfriendly, (noun) personal enemy
initium, -ī (n), beginning
iniūria, -ae (f), wrong, injury, offence
inopia, -ae (f), scarcity, want, lack
īnsidiae, -ārum (f pl), ambush, plot, snare
īnsigne, -is (n), mark, device
īnstituō, -uere (3), **-uī, -ūtum,** set up, establish, begin
īnstō, -āre (1), **-itī,** to press on, be at hand
īnstruō, -ere (3), **-xī, -ctum,** to draw up, equip
integer, -gra, -grum, whole, fresh, unbroken
intellegō, -gere (3), **-xī, -ctum,** to understand
intendō, -dere (3), **-dī, -tum,** to strive for, aim, intend
intentus, -a, -um, on the watch, vigilant
inter (+ acc.), between, among
intereā, meanwhile
interficiō, -ficere (3), **-fēcī, -fectum,** to kill
interim, meanwhile
*__interrogō__ (1), to question, interview, impeach, try
*__intestīnus, -a, -um,__ internal
intrā (+ acc.), within, inside of
*__invādō, -dere__ (3), **-sī, -sum,** to enter, assail, come over
inveniō, -enīre (4), **-ēnī, -entum,** to come upon, find, discover
*__invidia, -ae__ (f), envy, jealousy, unpopularity
invītus, -a, -um, unwilling
ipse, ipsa, ipsum, -self
īra, -ae (f), anger
is, ea, id, this, that, he, she, it
iste, ista, istud, that (of yours)
ita, so, in this way
*__itaque,__ and so, therefore
item, likewise
iter, -ineris (n), journey, march, road
iubeō, -bēre (2), **-ssī, -ssum,** to order
iūcundus, -a, -um, pleasing, delightful
*__iūdicium, -ī__ (n), court of law, trial
iūdicō (1), to judge
iungō, -gere (3), **xī, ctum,** to join
*__iūs, iūris__ (n) right, law, jurisdiction
*__iūre__ (abl.), rightly, justly

L

labor, -ōris (m), toil, hardship, work
labōrō (1), to work, struggle

lacessō, -ere (3), **-īvī, -ītum**, to harass, attack

laetitia, -ae (f), happiness, joy

laetus, -a, -um, happy, joyous, glad

*****latrō, -ōnis** (m), highwayman, gangster

latus, -eris (n), side, flank

laus, -dis (f), praise

lēgātus, -ī, (m), envoy, lieutenant

legiō, -ōnis (f), a legion

lēgō (1), to appoint

legō, -ere (3), **lēgī, lēctum**, to read, gather, choose, select

lēnis, -is, -e, mild, gentle

levis, -is, -e, light, unimportant

lēx, lēgis (f), law

libenter, willingly, gladly

līber, -era, -erum, free

līberī, -ōrum (m pl), children

līberō (1), to free

lībertās, -ātis (f), liberty, freedom

*****lībertus, -ī** (m), freedman

*****libīdō** (= **lubīdō**), **-inis** (f), pleasure, lust, passion

licet, -ēre (2), **-uit** (impersonal), it is permitted, one may

littera, -ae (f), letter (of alphabet), (pl.) epistle, letter

locus, -ī (m), place

    loca, -ōrum (n pl), region

longē, far

lūctus, -ūs (m), mourning, grief

M

maeror, -ōris (m), sadness

magis, more

magistrātus, -ūs (m), magistrate, magistracy

magnus, -a, -um, large

mālō, -lle (irreg.), **-luī**, to prefer

malus, -a, -um, bad

mando (1), to entrust, command

manus, -ūs (f), hand, band (of persons)

mare, -is (n), sea

maximus, -a, -um, very great, greatest, very large

mediocris, -is, -e, ordinary

    mediocriter, moderately, slightly

medius, -a, -um, mid-, middle part of

meminī, -inisse (irreg.), to remember

*****memor, -ris**, remembering, mindful

memoria, -ae (f), memory

*****memorō** (1), to recall, remember

mēns, -tis (f), mind

metus, -ūs (m), fear

meus, -a, -um, my

mīles, -itis (m), soldier

minuō, -uere (3), **-uī, -ūtum**, to diminish, lessen

minus, less

miser, -era, -erum, wretched, unhappy

misericordia, -ae (f), mercy, pity

mittō, -ere (3), **mīsī, missum**, to send

modo, only, just now, lately

modus, -ī (m), manner, way

*****moenia, -ium** (n pl), defenses, walls, city (enclosed by walls)

*****molior, -īrī** (4), **-ītus sum**, to attempt, undertake, plot

moneō (2), to warn, advise

mōns, -tis (m), mountain, hill

mora, -ae (f), delay

mors, -tis (f), death

mōs, mōris (m), custom, habit, (pl.) character

moveō, -ēre (2), **mōvī, mōtum**, to move

mulier, -eris (f), woman

*****multitūdō, -inis** (f), crowd, throng, host

multus, -a, -um, much, (pl.) many

*****mūnicipium, -ī** (n), free town

mūniō (4), to fortify, construct

mūrus, -ī (m), wall

N

nam, for

*****nārrō** (1), to tell, relate

nāscor, -ī (3), **nātus sum**, to be born

nātiō, -ōnis (f), tribe, race, nation

nātūra, -ae (f), nature

nē, that . . . not, lest, that

necessitās, -ātis (f), necessity, fate

necō (1), to kill

*****nefārius, -a, -um**, infamous, wicked, criminal

neglegō, -gere (3), **-xī, -ctum**, to neglect, disregard

negōtium, -ī (n), business, trouble

nēmō, nūllīus, no one

neque (= **nec**), and . . . not, neither, nor, but . . . not

    neque . . . neque, neither . . . nor

nēve (= **neu**), and . . . not, nor, and that not

*****nī** = **nisi**

nihil (n), nothing

*****nimis**, too much, too

nisi, unless, if . . . not

nōbilis, -is, -e, prominent, well-known, of high birth or rank

nōlō, -lle (irreg.), **-luī**, to be unwilling, not wish

nōmen, -inis (n), name, reputation

nōn, not

nōndum, not yet

nōnne . . . ? (introduces a question expecting the answer "yes")

nōnnūllī, -ae, -a (pl), some, a few, a number

nōscō, -scere (3), **nōvī, nōtum**, to come to know, (perfect) to know

noster, -tra, -trum, our, ours

novus, -a, -um, new

nox, -ctis (f), night

nūllus, -a, -um, no, not one

numerus, -ī (m), number

numquam, never

nūntius, -ī (m), message, messenger

O

ō, o! oh! alas!

ob (+ *acc.*), on account of

*__obnoxius__, **-a**, **-um**, subject to, submissive, under obligation to

obsideō, **-idēre** (2), **-ēdī**, **-essum**, to besiege

obtineō, **-inēre** (2), **-inuī**, **-entum**, to hold, occupy

occīdō, **-dere** (3), **-dī**, **-sum**, to kill

occultō (1), to hide

occultus, **-a**, **-um**, hidden

*__occultē__, secretly

occupō (1), to seize

oculus, **-ī** (*m*), eye

offerō, **offerre** (*irreg.*), **obtulī**, **oblātum**, to offer, present, expose

officium, **-ī** (*n*), duty, service

omittō, **-ittere** (3), **-īsī**, **-issum**, to disregard, let go

omnis, **-is**, **-e**, every, (pl.) all

onus, **-eris** (*n*), burden

opera, **-ae** (*f*), effort, services

oportet, **-ēre** (2), **-uit** (*impersonal*), it is right, (one) ought

opportūnus, **-a**, **-um**, favorable, opportune

opprimō, **-imere** (3), **-essī**, **-essum**, to crush, overwhelm

ops, **opis** (*f*), aid, (pl.) wealth, resources

optō (1), to choose, desire, pray for

opus est (+ *abl.*), there is need (for)

ōrātiō, **-ōnis** (*f*), speech

*__ōrdō__, **-inis** (*m*), rank, row, order, class

orior, **-īrī** (4), **ortus sum**, to rise, get up

   ortus, **-a**, **-um**, sprung from

ōrō (1), to beg, plead

ostendō, **-dere** (3), **-dī**, **-tum**, to show

P

parcō, **-cere** (3), **pepercī**, to spare

parēns, **-ntis** (*m/f*), parent

pāreō (2) (+ *dat.*), to obey

pariēs, **-etis** (*m*), wall

parō (1), to prepare, make ready

*__parricīda__, **-ae** (*m*), murderer, traitor

pars, **-tis** (*f*), part

parvus, **-a**, **-um**, small

*__patefaciō__, **-facere** (3), **-fēcī**, **-factum**, to lay open, reveal

pateō, **-ēre** (2), **-uī**, to extend, be open

pater, **-tris** (*m*), father

patior, **-tī** (3), **-ssus sum**, to allow, permit, suffer

*__patrēs cōnscrīptī__ (*m pl*), Fathers of the Senate

patria, **-ae** (*f*), homeland, native land

*__paucī__, **-ae**, **-a**, few, a few

paulātim, gradually, little by little

paulum, a little

*__paulō__, (by) a little

pāx, **pācis** (*f*), peace

pecūnia, **-ae** (*f*), money

pedes, **-itis** (*m*), foot soldier, (pl.) infantry

pendō, **-dere** (3), **pependī**, **-sum**, to pay, weigh

*__pēnsum__, **-ī** (*n*), a thing of weight, importance, or value

per (+ *acc.*), through

perdō, **-ere** (3), **-idī**, **-itum**, to destroy, lose

*__perditus__, **-a**, **-um**, ruined, reckless, abandoned

perīculum, **-ī** (*n*), danger

permittō, **-ittere** (3), **-īsī**, **-issum**, to entrust, permit

*__perniciēs__, **-ēī** (*f*), physical destruction, ruin

perspiciō, **-icere** (3), **-ēxī**, **-ectum**, to perceive, see through

perturbō (1), to confuse, disturb

pēs, **pedis** (*m*), foot

pessimus, **-a**, **-um**, worst, very bad

*__pestis__, **-is** (*f*), plague, ruin, destruction

petō, **-ere** (3), **-īvī**, **-ītum**, to seek, attack, be a candidate for

pīlum, **-ī** (*n*), javelin

placeō (2), to please

plēbs, **-ēbis** (*f*), the plebs, the common people

plērīque, **-aeque**, **-aque**, most, very many

poena, **-ae** (*f*), penalty, punishment

polliceor, **-ērī** (2), **-itus sum**, to promise

pōnō, **pōnere** (3), **posuī**, **positum**, to place, put, pitch (camp)

pōns, **-ntis** (*m*), bridge

*__populāris__, **-is** (*m/f*), associate, accomplice, confederate

populus, **-ī** (*m*), people, nation

porta, **-ae** (*f*), gate

portō (1), to carry

possideō, **-idēre** (2), **-ēdī**, **-essum**, to hold, possess

possum, **posse** (*irreg.*), **potuī**, to be able, can

post (+ *acc.*), after, behind

posteā, thereafter, afterward

postquam, after

*__postrēmō__, finally

postulō (1), to demand, ask

potēns, **-ntis**, powerful

potior, **-īrī** (4), **-ītus sum** (+ *abl.* or *gen.*), to get possession of

praecipiō, **-ipere** (3), **-ēpī**, **-eptum**, to instruct, advise, anticipate

praemium, **-ī** (*n*), reward

praesertim especially

praesidum, **-ī** (*n*), guard, garrison, protection

praestō, **-āre** (1), **-itī**, **-ātum**, to excel, show, be responsible for, (*impersonal*) it is better

praeter (+ *acc.*), beyond, except, besides

praetereā, besides that, furthermore

praetor, **-ōris** (*m*), praetor, judge

pretium, **-ī** (*n*), price, reward

prīmus, **-a**, **-um**, first, first part of

prīnceps, **-ipis** (*m*), chief, leading person, first to . . .

prior, **prius**, former

prīstinus, **-a**, **-um**, ancient, former

prius (*adv.*), earlier, before
priusquam, before, until
prīvātus, -a, -um, private
prīvō (1), to deprive
*__prō__ (+ *abl.*), before, for, in behalf of, in exchange for, in place of
*__prōcēdō, -dere__ (3), **-ssī, -ssum**, to advance, move forward
procul, from (or at) a distance, afar
prōdō, -ere (3), **-idī, -itum**, to betray, disclose, hand on
proelium, -ī (*n*), battle
profectō (*adv.*), surely, really
proficīscor, -icīscī (3), **-ectus sum**, to set out, start
*__properē__, hastily, speedily
propter (+ *acc.*), on account of, because of
*__prōvideō, -idēre__ (2), **-īdī, -īsum**, to see ahead, anticipate, prevent
prōvincia, -ae (*f*), province, sphere of duty
*__pūblicō__ (1), to make public property of
pūblicus, -a, -um, public, belonging to the people
pugna, -ae (*f*), fight
pugnō (1), to fight
pūniō (4), to punish
putō (1), to think

Q

quā, by which way, where
*__quam__ (+ *superlative*), as . . . as possible
quam, how, as, than
*__quamquam__, although, and yet
quantus, -a, -um, how great, (as great) as
*__quārē__, therefore, why
quārtus, -a, -um, fourth
*__quasi__, as if
-que, and
quī, quae, quod, who, which, that, what? which?
*__quia__, because, for
quīcumque, quaecumque, quodcumque, whoever, whichever, whatever
quīdam, quaedam, quiddam, certain, a certain
quidem, indeed, certainly, at least
quiēs, -ētis (*f*), rest, quiet
quiētus, -a, -um, quiet
quis, quid, anyone, anything, someone
quis, quid, who? what?
quisquam, quicquam (quidquam), anyone, anything
quisque, quaeque, quidque, each, each one
quisquis, quicquid, whoever, whatever
quō, to what place, whither
quoad, until, as long as
quod, because, as to the fact that, that
quodsī (quod sī), but if
quoniam, since, because
*__quō ūsque__, to what extent, how long?

R

*__rapīna, -ae__ (*f*), pillage, robbery, plundering
recūsō (1), to refuse
*__referō, -ferre__ (*irreg.*), **rettulī, relātum**, to bring back, refer
rēgnum, ī (*n*), reign, royal power, kingdom
relicuus (= reliquus), -a, -um, remaining, the rest of
relinquō, -inquere (3), **-īquī, -ictum**, to leave behind, abandon
*__removeō, -ovēre__ (2), **-ōvī, -ōtum**, to remove
*__reor, rērī__ (2), **ratus sum**, to think, have the opinion
repente, suddenly
reperiō, -īre (4), **repperī, -tum**, to find, find out
reprehendō, -dere (3), **-dī, -sum**, to blame, censure
repudiō (1), reject
rēs, reī (*f*), thing, matter, affair
respondeō, -dēre (2), **-dī, -sum**, to reply, answer
rēspūblica, reīpūblicae (*f*), the state, government
rēx, rēgis (*m*), king
rogō (1), to ask

S

saepe, often
salūs, -ūtis (*f*), safety
salvus, -a, -um, safe
sapiēns, -ntis, wise, (noun) philosopher
satis, enough, sufficiently
satisfaciō, -facere (3), **-fēcī, -factum**, to satisfy, do one's duty (to)
scelerātus, -a, -um, criminal
*__scelus, -eris__ (*n*), crime
sciō (4), to know
scrībō, -bere (3), **-psī, -ptum**, to write, enroll (troops)
sē: see **suī**
sed, but
sēdēs, -is (*f*), seat, home, abode
semper, always
senātus, -ūs (*m*), Senate
sententia, -ae (*f*), opinion
sentiō, -tīre (4), **-sī, -sum**, to feel, perceive, think
sequor, -quī (3), **-cūtus sum**, to follow
sermō, -ōnis (*m*), talk, conversation
*__servitium, ī__ (*n*), servitude, slavery, (pl.) slaves
servō (1), to save, guard, keep safe
sī, if
sīcut (= sīcutī), as if, just as
signum, -ī (*n*), sign, signal, standard
similis, -is, -e, like, similar
simul, at the same time
sīn, but if

sine (+ abl.), without
singulāris, -is, -e, unique
singulī, -ae, -a, one at a time, one each
sīve ... sīve (= seu ... seu), whether ...
or
socius, -ī (m), ally, associate
*soleō, -ēre (2), -itus sum, to be accustomed
sollicitō (1), to stir up, bribe
sōlum, only
sōlus, -a, -um, lone, only, alone
spatium, -ī (n), space, interval
spectō (1), to watch, look at
spērō (1), to hope
spēs, speī (f), hope
spīritus, -ūs (m), breath
spoliō (1), to strip, rob
statuō, -uere (3), -uī, -ūtum, to set, decide,
determine
stīpendium, ī (n), pay, tribute
*strēnuus, -a, -um, energetic
*studium, -ī (n), eagerness, zeal, enthusiasm
sub (+ acc. or abl.), under
subsidium, -ī (n), reinforcement
suī, sibi, sē, himself, herself, itself, themselves
sum, esse (irreg.), fuī, futūrus, to be
summa, -ae (f), sum, total, main part,
supremacy
summus, -a, -um, highest (part of)
sūmō, -mere (3), -mpsī, -mptum, to take,
assume
*superbia, -ae (f), haughtiness, arrogance
superior, -ius, higher, former, preceding
superō (1), to conquer, overpower, surpass
supplicium, -ī (n), punishment, torture
  supplicium sūmere (+ dē + abl.), to
  impose the (death) penalty on
suprā, above, before
suscipiō, -ipere (3), -ēpī, -eptum, to undertake
suus, -a, -um, his (own), hers, its, their

T

*taeter, -tra, -trum, offensive, foul, loathsome
*tālis, -is, -e, such, of such a kind
tam, so, so very
tamen, however
tandem, at last, finally
*tantum, only, merely
tantus, -a, -um, so great, so much
*tēctum, -ī (n), roof, building, house
tegō, -gere (3), -xī, -ctum, cover, protect
tēlum, -ī (n), weapon, missile
temere, rashly, blindly
tempestās, -ātis (f), weather, storm, occasion, crisis
templum, -ī (n), temple
temptō (1), to test, try
tempus, -oris (n), time
tendō, -dere (3), tetendī, -tum, to stretch,
lay (out)

tenebrae, -ārum (f pl), darkness
teneō, -ēre (2), -uī, -tum, to hold, keep
terra, -ae (f), earth, land
tertius, -a, -um, third
Tiberis, -is (m/f), the river Tiber
timeō (2), to fear
*timor, -ōris (m), fear
tollō, -ere (irreg.), sustulī, sublātum, to
raise, lift, remove
tōtus, -a, -um, all, whole, entire
trādō, -ere (3), -idī, -itum, to hand over,
hand down
Trānsalpīnus, -a, -um, across the Alps (to
the north of Italy)
trānsferō, -ferre (irreg.), -tulī, -lātum, to
carry over
trēs, trēs, tria, three
triumphus, -ī (m), a triumph, triumphal
procession
tū, vōs, you
tueor, -ērī (2), tuitus (tūtus) sum, to defend,
guard
tum, then
tumultus, -ūs (m), uproar, riot, uprising
tūtus, -a, -um, safe
tuus, -a, -um, your, yours

U

ubi, when, where, in which place
ūllus, -a, -um, any
ūnā (adv.), together
unde, from which place
undique, everywhere, on all sides
ūniversus, -a, -um, whole, entire
ūnus, -a, -um, one
urbs, - bis (f), city
ūsus, -ūs (m), use, experience
  ūsus est, there is need
ut (= utī), that, as, when
uterque, utraque, utrumque, each (of two),
both
*utī = ut
ūtilis, -is, -e, useful
ūtor, -ī (3), ūsus sum (+ abl.), to use

V

vacuus, -a, -um, empty
valeō (2), to be strong
*vānus, -a, -um, worthless
*varius, -a, -um, varied, different
vastō (1), to lay waste, devastate
vehemēns, -ntis, violent, severe
vel ... vel, either ... or
veniō, venīre (4), vēnī, ventum, to come
vereor, -ērī (2), -itus sum, to fear, respect
*vērō, indeed, truly, in fact
versor (1), to be occupied with, dwell, be
*vērum, but
vērus, -a, -um, true
vester (= voster), -tra, -trum, your, yours

vetō, **-āre** (1), **-uī**, **-itum**, to forbid
vetus, (*gen.*) **-eris**, old
*****vexō** (1), to annoy, ravage
victor, **-ōris** (*m*), victor, conqueror
victōria, **-ae** (*f*), victory
vīcus, **ī** (*m*), village, street, district, ward (of a city)
vidēlicet, doubtless, evidently
videō, **vidēre** (2), **vīdī**, **vīsum**, to see
videor, **-ērī** (2), **vīsus sum**, to seem, appear
*****vigilia**, **-ae** (*f*), watch (of the night), sentry, (usually pl.) wakefulness
vīlla, **-ae** (*f*), country house, estate, villa
vincō, **-ere** (3), **vīcī**, **victum**, to conquer
vinculum, **ī** (*n*), chain, fetter, bond
vir, **virī** (*m*), man
virtūs, **-ūtis** (*f*), courage
vīs, **vim**, **vī** (*f*), force, violence, (pl.) strength

vīta, **-ae** (*f*), life
vītō (1), to avoid, shun
vīvō, **-ere** (3), **-xī**, **-ctum**, to live
vīvus, **-a**, **-um**, alive, living
vocō (1), to call
volgus (= **vulgus**), **-ī** (*n*), the common people
volnerō (= **vulnerō**) (1), to wound, injure
volnus (= **vulnus**), **eris** (*n*), wound
volō, **velle** (*irreg.*), **voluī**, to will, be willing, want, wish
voltus (= **vultus**), **-ūs** (*m*), face, expression
voluntās, **-ātis** (*f*), wish, will, goodwill
*****volvō**, **-vere** (3), **-vī**, **-ūtum**, to turn over, roll over
voster: see **vester**
vōx, **vōcis** (*f*), voice, word
*****vultus**: see **voltus**

CREDITS

TEXT CREDITS AND SOURCES

Pages 70–71: From *Historia*, "Iusta Catalinae" by Robin Seager, © 1973 by Franz Steiner Verlag; reprinted by permission of Robin Seager. Pages 72–73: From *The Conspiracy of Catiline* by Lester Hutchinson; Barnes & Noble Inc., © 1967 by Anthony Blond. Pages 73–74: From *The History of Rome* by Theodor Mommsen, translated by W.P. Dickson, © by J.M. Dent & Sons Ltd. Pages 74–75: From *The Catilinarian Conspiracy in its Context* by E.G. Hardy, © 1976; reprinted by Ams Press, Inc., New York. Pages 75–76: From *The History of Rome* by Theodor Mommsen, translated by W.P. Dickson, © by J.M. Dent & Sons Ltd. Page 77: From *The Conspiracy of Catiline* by Lester Hutchinson; Barnes & Noble Inc., © 1967 by Anthony Blond.

PHOTOS

Page 2: From *A History of Rome*, Third Edition, by M. Cary and H.H. Scullard. Published in the United States by St. Martin's Press, copyright © 1975. Used with permission of publisher. Page 5: From *Cicero, First & Second Speeches Against Catiline* edited by H.E. Gould and J.L. Whiteley, © 1982 by Bristol Classical Press. Page 19: Alinari/Art Resource, NY. Pages 30, 31: Fototeca Unione, at the American Academy in Rome. Page 33: Alinari/Art Resource, NY. Page 35: From *A History of Rome*, Third Edition, by M. Cary and H.H. Scullard. Published in the United States by St. Martin's Press, copyright © 1975. Pages 38, 39: Fototeca Unione, at the American Academy in Rome. Page 42: Fototeca Unione, at the American Academy in Rome. Page 54: Reproduced by Courtesy of the Trustees of the British Museum; From the Musée Archeologique de Rabat, Maroc. Page 55: Alinari/Art Resource, NY. Page 60: The Mansell Collection Ltd. Page 63: From *Greece and Rome at War* by Peter Connolly, © 1981 by Prentice-Hall Inc. Page 64: Staatliche Antikensammlungen Und Glyptothek. Pages 65, 67: From *Greece and Rome at War* by Peter Connolly, © 1981 by Prentice-Hall Inc.